LinkedIn for me and my career or business

Tried and True
Tips and Techniques

Sue Ellson

Published by

120 Ways Publishing PO Box 65, Surrey Hills, Victoria, Australia, 3127
info@120wayspublishing.com sueellson@sueellson.com

Printed by
IngramSpark 76 Discovery Road Dandenong South, Victoria,
Australia, 3175 ingramsparkinternational@ingramcontent.com

National Library of Australia Cataloguing-in-Publication entry

Ellson, Sue, 1965 – Author

LinkedIn for me and my career or business, Tried and
True Tips and Techniques / Sue Ellson

ISBN-10: 0-6484775-0-1 ISBN 13: 978-0-6484775-0-1 (paperback)
eBook (ePub and PDF) available

Includes index. Books – Careers, Career Development, Business, Self-Help

Please note

All care has been taken in the preparation of this book. The publisher and the author have no liability to any person or entity with respect to any loss or damage alleged to have been caused directly or indirectly by the information contained herein, which was correct at the time of writing, and is based on Sue Ellson's acquired experience, but is subject to change.

All information is of a general nature and does not take into account your personal circumstances and is therefore not advice. This personally created content has not been written, approved or endorsed by any assistive tool, individual or enterprize. Trademark information has been omitted from the main text to assist readability. All trademarked brands are owned by their respective corporations. Sue Ellson does not have any personal or financial affiliation or accreditation from LinkedIn or Microsoft.

Dedication

For my children and the people
who have believed in me.

Reviews

If you are ready to get serious about LinkedIn this book is your step by step guide. Sue has given so many expert tips to ensure you are set up for success. Whether it's reviewing your existing LinkedIn Profile set up or looking for guidance to get started this book is for you. Sue has done a brilliant job in not just explaining what to do, but why you should do it. *Michelle J Raymond LinkedIn B2B Trainer - Good Trading Co*

This is the only comprehensive book you require whether commencing your LinkedIn journey or maximising your LinkedIn information to maximize the potential to reach your optimal career goal or enhance your business opportunities. This sophisticated tool explains clearly and with the experience developed over a significant number of years, all you want to know and if you want help you can contact Sue directly. Sue's poem called 'LinkedIn' before the Introduction summarises the experiences and opportunities you will have working with this book. Go ahead and enjoy! *Suzanne Dunlop, Chairperson, Neighbourhood Watch (Not for Profit), Melbourne, Victoria, Australia*

Complete, to-the-point, extremely pragmatic and packed with valuable insights to boost your career. Whether you are actively searching or just a latent job seeker, this is a MUST read. *Richard van der Blom, Global LinkedIn Thought Leader and Trainer on Social and Virtual Selling, Maastricht, Limburg, Netherlands*

If you have ever said to yourself, "I keep hearing about LinkedIn, but I don't how it can benefit me, or where to begin," this books is for you. Sue Ellson's up to date, straightforward guide covers many of the questions that come up frequently during coaching sessions. She eloquently toggles between strategy and hands on tactics to make sure the reader gets the knowledge and tools needed to reach their goals using LinkedIn effectively. A tremendous resource! *Hannah Tighe, LinkedIn Training and Coaching Specialist, Douglassville, Pennsylvania, USA*

Extremely comprehensive. Congratulations on your dedication to writing this, and pouring your knowledge into it. I hope people will read it and TAKE ACTION. *Mark Stonham, Bristol, England, United Kingdom*

This is a comprehensive guide about LinkedIn. Sue's writing style will make you feel like she's there with you. Recommended reading. *Karen Hollenbach, LinkedIn Training Specialist, Melbourne, Victoria, Australia*

Don't miss Sue's excellent book, 'LinkedIn for me and my career or Business.' It's chock full of actionable and valuable advice in a very relaxed and personable style.' *Sid Clark, Independent LinkedIn Trainer and Coach, Lake Forest, California, USA*

'LinkedIn for me and my career or Business' has some great insights on how LinkedIn works in a two-way street. *Barry Jenner, Management Consultant, Melbourne, Australia*

Sue Ellson's latest book, 'LinkedIn for me and my career or business' would be ideal for people who run their own business, who are searching for work, looking for volunteering opportunities or are wanting an encore career. It's well set out and is full of good, practical, detailed information. *Jill Weeks, Pre & Post Retirement Content Creator, Melbourne, Victoria, Australia*

'LinkedIn for me and my career or business' digs deep into the fundamentals of LinkedIn, both the why and the how, spelling out essential best practices for successfully using LinkedIn, regardless of your role or current business goals. *Scott Allen, CEO/Author The Virtual Handshake*

Sue is a LinkedIn master who has comprehensively shared her tips, knowledge and experience on how to use LinkedIn to enhance your personal brand and accentuate your career. Well worth reading. *Chris J. "Mohawk" Reed, CEO & Founder of Black Marketing-The Dark Art of Social Media Marketing, Singapore, Singapore*

Sue Ellson's understanding of the practical, effective and ethical utilisation of LinkedIn is extraordinary as evidenced by the comprehensive material in this book and by appropriate clients accessing my services via LinkedIn. Also, thanks to Sue's knowledge of the considered use of social media, I am at the top in Google searches and appear five times in the top six results. *John McCann, Executive Coach and Registered Psychologist, Brisbane, Queensland, Australia*

Informative reviews welcome at

https://120wayspublishing.com/books/book-reviews-of-LinkedIn-for-me-and-my-career-or-business or

https://www.goodreads.com/sueellson

https://g.page/sue-ellson-author/review

https://sueellson.com/reviews

Acknowledgements

Enduring thanks over many years for the constant love, support and faith in my abilities to Suzanne Dunlop, some very special personal friends, business friends and long term clients. Thank you for believing in me.

Thanks and kudos to all of my clients (from individuals to people in large enterprizes), students, LinkedIn peers, fellow career development practitioners, business coaches, LinkedIn connections, authors and writers for your questions and perspectives that have challenged me to always dig deeper and find the best tips and techniques for more people.

Thanks to Boja from 99 Designs and Gefferson Heemann for their assistance with the cover design. Thanks to Sid Clark for his pro bono editing services.

Thanks to you, the reader, for investing in yourself. I now encourage you to read on and start getting excited about how you can make LinkedIn work for you and your work, career, business or enterprize.

Quick disclaimer: *All of the content in this book revised and published in 2023 is based on my personal experience and use of LinkedIn since 2003 and consulting and training services I have provided since 2008. It is designed for general informational purposes. It is not professional advice for your personal circumstances.*

Other LinkedIn trainers and advisers will have their own strategies for using LinkedIn and if it differs to what I have suggested here, I encourage you to ask them 'why' they make their recommendations and I would then encourage you to make the decisions that are right for you and your goals provided they are in accordance with the LinkedIn User Agreement https://www.linkedin.com/legal/user-agreement.

Discernment is essential, but please don't wait for perfection - it doesn't exist. Your LinkedIn Profile is only ever a version number that can be changed at a later date. As an Educator, Practitioner and Consultant, I have adopted a teaching format to my writing that allows you to build on what you may already know with practical examples.

You are welcome to visit my LinkedIn Profile at any time to see how I use LinkedIn https://www.linkedin.com/in/sueellson.

You may also find that my first book on LinkedIn, '120 Ways To Achieve Your Purpose With LinkedIn' may be helpful to you as it includes a range of different information. Think of the first book as the 'LinkedIn Strategy Manifesto' and this book as the 'User Guide.'

I strongly recommend that you complement your learnings with online courses available at https://sueellson.com/courses.

Why Is This Book Helpful?

If you take action, it will help you

1. Clarify and achieve your goals, purpose and objectives.
2. Record and reflect on your achievements and impacts to date.
3. Attract aligned opportunities or maintain your status.
4. Quantify your improvements through a change in your statistics.
5. Self-select aligned strategies and tactics for your career or business.
6. Create a high quality optimized digital asset.
7. Revise your strategies as you change.
8. Focus on what will work best for you.
9. Showcase your improved digital competency.
10. Assist you at a personal and professional level.

This is book is not designed to read on a comfortable lounge chair, sipping your favorite beverage (unless you enjoy a quick skim read first).

I encourage you to 'read' this book by highlighting, recording or completing your action tasks on a laptop or desktop computer as you go along and that way you will see results, possibly even sooner than you expect. Keep your Mobile Phone handy too.

It is also much easier to do the work in small chunks or with a friend.

Clarifying your goals, purpose and objectives first is ideal, but if you are not 100% sure of what you would like to do next, simply record what you have done up until now in your LinkedIn Profile and then go back to the clarification process later. Some people find that as they record what they have already done, even if it takes more than 10 hours, they become much clearer about their next steps. Reflection leads to clarification.

I would also like to add that if you take action, you are more likely to be completing aligned tasks, with aligned people in an aligned location for an aligned remuneration. Every step you complete is one step closer.

I often say, just because you know how to do a job (work), it doesn't mean you know how to get a job (work). This book provides tried and tested tips and techniques that you can use. I sincerely hope you have fun, enjoy the process and achieve the outcomes you desire.

Contents

Preface

I am passionate about connecting people and making sure that they can communicate with one another. Of all of the skills I have acquired over the years, this concept is what drives my dedication, commitment, learning and output.

When I wrote and independently published my first book, '120 Ways To Achieve Your Purpose With LinkedIn,' I was able to compile and curate all that I had learnt into a LinkedIn Strategy Manifesto. The process was cathartic. At the time, I was very much a 'Sue Everything' type of person, but writing the book helped me realize that LinkedIn was a tool that could be used for so many different purposes and for so many different people.

My second book, '120 Ways To Attract The Right Career Or Business' allowed me to share relevant stories from many different people that I hoped the reader could relate to and apply to their own journey.

My third book, '120 Ways To Market Your Business Hyper Locally' was case study driven, because everyone in business wants to know what works.

My fourth book 'Gigsters - Any Age or Ability Employees, Experts and Entrepreneurs' allowed me to create a methodology that many different types of people could use to live their purpose.

For too long, people have been criticized for not following traditional conventions and I wanted to give people a language to describe their choices. In the future world of work, many more people will need to adopt the gigster mindset and use technology to attract aligned opportunities.

Of these first four books, my most popular one was the first! That tells me something...that people are starting to realize the value of LinkedIn. However, the first book was very detailed and extremely comprehensive and focused on strategy more than tactics.

This book combines both - strategy and tactics and is designed to be immediately actionable for people of all ages and abilities.

It includes a huge range of updates from the first book because LinkedIn has introduced so many new features. This is another reason why I find LinkedIn so valuable for either a career or business, because it caters for both.

If you are part of a not-for-profit, government, professional association or other enterprize, the business suggestions will also apply to you.

I encourage you to read from the very beginning as your own LinkedIn Profile is an essential component to your success on LinkedIn.

'LinkedIn for me and my career or business' is for:

- understanding how you can use LinkedIn effectively
- clarifying your values, strengths and context
- effectively engaging with people and content
- curating and creating relevant content
- attracting the right career or business
- sourcing the right leads, sales and results
- ethically achieving your goals and outcomes
- creating and maintaining a network of opportunities and referrals
- making the right choices for you

It includes information for:

- students, job seekers and career changers
- freelancers, gigsters, entrepreneurs and business owners
- tradespeople and specialist practitioners
- advisors, consultants and thought leaders
- community groups and professional associations
- not-for-profit collectives, groups and enterprizes
- schools, colleges and universities
- career specialists and social media professionals

This book will help you complete your LinkedIn Profile and LinkedIn Page and teach you how to use LinkedIn to develop your network, maintain those relationships with semi-frequent activity, attract aligned individuals and opportunities and achieve your career and business goals both now and in the future. At all times, it will focus on actionable, ethical and respectful practice.

Get started and take action now!

** Online courses at https://sueellson.com/courses

LinkedIn

Profiling

Connecting

Engaging

Curating

Creating

Publishing

Attracting

Distracting

Meeting

Learning

Performing

Rewarding

Reviewing

Modifying

Exploring

Diversifying

Captivating

Networking

Referring

Remaining

Sue Ellson

Introduction

Are you at a crossroads with your career? Not sure what to do next or desperately seeking a new role? Do you have a business or enterprize that needs new leads, sales or results? Are you looking for a way to attract career or business opportunities without going through the process of applying for jobs or cold calling?

If nothing changes, nothing changes. But how do you decide what to say and do on LinkedIn, especially if you are reluctant to put yourself out there publicly and are a bit nervous about what might happen if you do?

If you are a bit more confident and have already completed most sections of your LinkedIn Profile, are you attracting as many aligned career or business opportunities as you would like? Have you missed any opportunities that you could have had?

Can your LinkedIn network of Connections back you up in a time of crisis? You may have heard the saying, 'it is not what you know, it is who you know.' In my view, 'it is how you can be referred or found and verified' that counts. If you want to get the right job, be promoted, start a side hustle, business or social enterprize, you can start with a free LinkedIn Profile.

Did you know that most people will Google you before reaching out to you and that LinkedIn is highly optimized for online name searches?

How can you encourage the right decision-makers to contact you (or not contact you and just do what you suggest instead)? How can you showcase the value you offer and attract aligned opportunities whilst simultaneously discouraging unaligned opportunities?

How can you evaluate the effectiveness of your LinkedIn activity and select the most appropriate LinkedIn strategies for your goals?

Put simply, how can you get the results YOU want from LinkedIn?

1. Setup It all starts with creating a fully completed, keyword optimized LinkedIn Profile (and Page or School Page if you are representing an enterprize) that is aligned with your values, strengths and context.

2. Shine Once you understand algorithms, search queries and hacks, you can choose the right content and engagement strategies and get the results you want, in most cases, in less than 20 minutes a week.

3. Surprise To be memorable, you need to do things 'your way.' I would love to see more 'courageous characters' online. I don't mean attention seeking, click bait seekers. I mean respectful people who bring their unique perspective and style to the LinkedIn platform (or online more generally).

This practical book will help you choose what will work best for you and if you change your values, purpose, goals or objectives in the future, you can simply adjust your LinkedIn strategy and keep moving forward.

I personally believe that LinkedIn offers the most value out of all social media platforms currently available (and possibly in the future as I cannot see how any other platform could 'catch up' with the number of people with established LinkedIn Profiles on LinkedIn).

That said, I recommend that you choose other aligned social media platforms as well to achieve your goals. I have found that my own name website https://sueellson.com allows me full control over content and layout and is a great way to keep an archive of my online activity (and I regularly link to my social media posts from multiple platforms and often include a YouTube video on blog posts).

My first book, '120 Ways To Achieve Your Purpose With LinkedIn' summarized everything I had learnt about LinkedIn at that time.

This book has been written to help you achieve your work, career, business or enterprize goals. It provides strategies and tactics to help you (and possibly your clients) showcase your values, strengths and context via the LinkedIn platform and attract aligned opportunities on an ongoing basis as well as build your own network so that you can keep going through any crisis.

It is written in an ethical, respectful and practical way to help you use LinkedIn within the terms of the LinkedIn User Agreement (a direct link to the LinkedIn User Agreement is available in the footer of every page on LinkedIn) https://www.linkedin.com/legal/user-agreement (Section 8 on the Do's and Don'ts is essential reading). I feel very strongly about abiding by the LinkedIn User Agreement.

This book incorporates the most relevant concepts from my previous four books as they apply to LinkedIn and what I see as the future of work – where we will all have 'work' but not necessarily full time jobs or just one type of business or source of income.

I am always hopeful that the future will enable you to be your 'own kind of peculiar' and enable you to bring your unique talents and abilities to your local and international community as a 'citizen of the world' (from my book *Gigsters - Any Age or Ability Employees, Experts and Entrepreneurs*).

I encourage you to be a 'courageous character.'

After joining LinkedIn on 21 December 2003 (User number 77,832), I have seen the platform grow and develop. Various features have been added and removed and I expect this constant updating to continue.

I started consulting on the topic of LinkedIn as an Independent LinkedIn Specialist on 10 November 2008. My first client still keeps me updated on their career and has inspired me with their various transitions and success stories over many years. For the record, I have never worked for LinkedIn, I do not have any personal or professional affiliation with LinkedIn and I have not been paid by anyone to write this book or include any particular content. This book has been exclusively written by me, the author. I have not used any assistive technology or artificial intelligence to prepare the content.

At the time of writing, LinkedIn's mission is to: *Connect the world's professionals to allow them to be more productive and successful.*

Unless mentioned otherwise, **all of the suggestions in the book are based on logging into LinkedIn on your laptop or desktop computer**. The LinkedIn app for phones and tablets is different and does not have the same functionality but there are special features available via the LinkedIn App that will be covered.

Some tips and techniques are mentioned more than once in case you skip to a specific section rather than read the entire book.

I believe that everyone should consider creating a LinkedIn Profile, their own personal website and a Google Business Account to establish their online digital footprint from the age of 16 until death. More about that later. Let's focus on your LinkedIn Profile first and get right into it!

1. What Is LinkedIn?

LinkedIn is currently the world's largest international online network of individuals from across the globe.

Originally launched in May 2003 and acquired by Microsoft in June 2016, it has developed from its original concept of being a network of professionals into a formidable publishing platform, a respected social media site (on both desktop/laptop and mobile phone/tablet) and a lead generation, sales and recruitment resource that has completely disrupted online selling and recruitment selection methodologies with its ability to attract opportunities within LinkedIn and via Search Engines (in particular, Google).

I am very pleased to see that LinkedIn includes many usability features that allow people of all abilities and backgrounds to access useful information either with or without assistive technology. This universal design principle can be of significant benefit to you and other LinkedIn Users if you complete your LinkedIn Profile or Page in full with text, images, audio and video and engage with the content in the Newsfeed, Articles, Newsletters, Events and Groups.

There has been a significant increase in the number of new features added to LinkedIn on a regular basis as a result of the many requests from LinkedIn Users and the competition they face from other social media platforms. The information in this book was current at the time of publication.

The specific links and settings may change but you will find that in most cases, the strategies mentioned here will last a lot longer.

As a freemium model offering limited free access to millions of users, it has acquired users across diverse industries and is particularly popular with well-educated white collar professionals.

1.1 LinkedIn Network

There are plenty of opportunities available for various professionals on LinkedIn including gigsters, tradespeople, academics, writers, artists, journalists and people who have a significant public profile.

I truly believe that our personal and financial security comes from the quality of our personal networks (the people we either know or can reach) and our ability to use our income for both asset and wealth creation (not just weekly expenses).

Our life can change at any time without notice, but if we have a network, we can find a way to carry on. This is very important for people going from a 'hero to zero' situation. This could include changing locations, suddenly losing a job, a business, your health or your status. Despite any of these challenges, there is always someone who can help.

Dunbar's number suggests that the number of stable social relationships we can cognitively maintain is between 150 and 250 people. LinkedIn enables us to have 30,000 people in our individual LinkedIn network and allows us to search for or be found by millions more. This gives us much greater access to more people, Companies and Schools. This helps us find people and be found by people, without us having to know those people. We can also have an unlimited number of Followers.

If we have just one source of income and we lose that source of income and do not have our own back up financial resources, we may find ourselves in an uncertain economic situation.

Even if we have adequate financial resources in the event of a crisis, we may still want to find ways to contribute either locally or internationally and may miss out on opportunities if we do not have an online presence that allows people to 'verify' us with their own personal online search (LinkedIn is much more than an online résumé or curriculum vitae/CV).

I believe it is not what you know or who you know, it is who or what (e.g. a search engine) can refer or find you and how your details can be verified that determines whether or not you will secure opportunities. LinkedIn provides you with an opportunity to be found and verified 24 hours a day, seven days a week across the globe – either as an individual or as an enterprize.

1.2 LinkedIn Features

LinkedIn has adapted and changed many times over the years. I have seen various features come and go. I will discuss the current most useful features for your career or business in this book. Some of these features may change in the future but the strategy usually remains.

Some of the current features have been acquired from other developers (like the Newsfeed from Pulse) and others have been developed in-house based on concepts that have started on other social media platforms (like #hashtags and @mentions from Twitter and Boosting of Posts from Facebook). Some features are more useful than others and some can be very time consuming and not generate a reasonable return for your time, effort or financial investment.

The platform was originally very robust technologically speaking and over the years, as more and more features have been added, there have been intermittent bugs and challenges that can confuse users who are not technologically savvy. For example, you could be trying to update some information and try and save the new information and then it suddenly freezes and doesn't allow the save to occur. You may need to be patient.

I mention this not to criticize LinkedIn but to help you understand that if something isn't working, it may be a technological issue rather than a user issue and it may be worth refreshing the screen or starting again tomorrow (and to avoid any loss of information, develop a good strategy of copying and saving any information in your own files before relying on your LinkedIn save request). Also, most new features are rolled out on a gradual basis across different locations which means that some users may have a new feature before other users.

I have written this book with a focus on LinkedIn. What you will realize is that you will be able to use most of the strategies for your personal or enterprize website, your other social media platforms and written, audio or video content that you publish online.

I am providing strategic information that helps you understand the logic of the LinkedIn platform and anything that relies on technology to do the heavy lifting for you. The tactics can also be re-used elsewhere on other online platforms and technologies.

At all times, I encourage you to be ethically responsible and respectfully considerate of other people, their privacy and personal reasons for having a public LinkedIn Profile. LinkedIn is designed to be a professional network and not a dating website or spam tool! LinkedIn has a number of systems in place to detect and cease unwanted or inappropriate behavior.

2. LinkedIn Offering

During in-person training, I find that most students and clients want to get straight to immediate results. That is perfectly understandable if securing a paid opportunity as soon as possible is a high priority for you right now.

Making direct contact with people you already know or visiting local businesses and offering your services is probably the fastest way to securing paid work at short notice (but don't forget, they are likely to look you up online before offering you the actual work either before an interview or before providing a written job offer).

If you don't understand how LinkedIn can help you, it is possible to overlook the various ways you can attract the right opportunities. You could also miss out on the most effective strategies that can help you achieve your goals. My goal is to teach you how to use the technology more effectively.

Ironically, **most people I meet already believe they know how to use LinkedIn because they have created a Profile and have filled in some sections**.

LinkedIn is way more than a tool to list information publicly. If you do not complete your LinkedIn Profile in full, you risk securing work that is not aligned either personally or financially. If you showcase your value more effectively, you have the potential to secure aligned work with aligned people in an aligned location for an aligned remuneration.

Whether you are looking for career or business opportunities, I always recommend a multiple concurrent strategy approach. This means using several strategies all at the same time rather than relying on one particular strategy before trying the next one (like applying for more than one job at a time rather than waiting to hear back from each application).

Likewise for business leads, there are many different strategies that can be used instead of the commonly used 'connect and pitch' approach that infuriates so many LinkedIn Users.

LinkedIn is a form of social media, so you need to complete your LinkedIn Profile, engage and offer value. Remember that it is important to listen and engage before speaking and asking for a sale.

Let's say you immediately need some sales. Rather than spending money on advertising, I would suggest that you reconnect with all of the people who have previously purchased your goods or services (existing customers or clients) and invite them to see your latest offerings. The relationship has already been developed and it is much easier to sell to a former happy client (or request a referral) than it is to sell to a brand new person who has never heard from you before.

This strategy worked very well for a client of mine. He had some time out as a result of receiving some medical treatment (he made a full recovery) but during that time, several pieces of ongoing work were cancelled and several clients postponed their next appointment.

I helped him draft an 'update' message that he personally sent to selected individuals and former clients. He could have also asked for referrals to other people they may know. Anyway, within two weeks, he had more work from his past clients than he could handle. This was far more effective than creating a paid advertising campaign to new prospects he has never contacted previously.

2.1 Benefits Of LinkedIn

Let's have a look at some of the many ways you can use LinkedIn.

- **An international cloud based personal database** – that allows you to have one source of truth for all of your Connections (if they have a LinkedIn Profile). LinkedIn Users automatically update their LinkedIn Profile so you don't have to maintain a separate database and update it every time someone changes their contact information, job role or business information. No more re-writing your list of contacts in your paper diary each year, creating a spreadsheet of your contacts or establishing a sophisticated database – just look up the details online or on your phone and contact people directly. Remember that so many email mailing lists become out of date very quickly – but if you connect via LinkedIn, you can always look someone up online. It could be a good idea to add a link to a person's LinkedIn URL in your customer relationship management CRM system or database so you can look them up directly if they change their contact details (and saves you searching for them too). This strategy is particularly relevant for alumni.

- **Digital business card** – I recommend that you **invite everyone you meet, from now on,** to connect with you on LinkedIn. This is very easy to do with the Scan Code feature from the Search Box in the LinkedIn App but you can also add your LinkedIn URL to your email signature, résumé or CV, phone contact details, website, printed or digital business card etc.

- **A network maintenance system** – I have heard of countless examples of people reconnecting with people they know by searching on LinkedIn or alternatively, securing ongoing referrals as a result of engaging with Posts or publishing their own Articles, Newsletters, Events or other content on LinkedIn. Some people have built bespoke international networks by adding new Connections to their network through online and offline techniques. An active presence on LinkedIn reminds people that you exist without you needing to personally contact each person on a regular basis to let them know that you are still alive.

- **A way to secure search engine results** – for your name, business or enterprize name, your keywords and more. LinkedIn is so well optimized in the Google search engine for peoples' names. It took me six months to get my exact match domain name https://sueellson.com above my LinkedIn Profile URL in local Google search engine results. Your LinkedIn Articles can also be optimized to potentially appear on page one of search engine results. I have several LinkedIn Articles in this spot.

- **A quick and easy contact tool** – if you include your contact details in several sections of your LinkedIn Profile, it is much easier for people to contact you (in the Contact Info section first, but you can also consider the About section and current Experience sections. It is important to keep your message clear so that if the person visiting your LinkedIn Profile only wants free information, they know where to go and if they want to engage professionally, they know how to do that too. If you have a very senior role, you may like to direct them to an online Enquiry Form via a URL link so that the person reaching out needs to provide more details before being able to contact you directly. This means you will not need to disclose your email address or phone number publicly. If you have safety concerns, please do not include your phone number anywhere on your LinkedIn Profile and use the Authenticator App or two factor authentication 2FA when logging in.

- **Online résumé or curriculum vitae CV** – LinkedIn creates an online framework for documenting your working life that is far more effective than a three page résumé or CV. By fully completing and updating your LinkedIn Profile and reflecting on your past experience, you may develop insights into your future direction. It is also a great way to catalogue information before you create your own personal website that showcases all of your previous work. Some employers have now made it mandatory to have a LinkedIn Profile as part of the job application process (in particular, for university graduates applying for internships). In other words, if you don't have a LinkedIn Profile, you will not get a job interview. Some new one-person solopreneur enterprizes start their ventures with nothing more than a LinkedIn Profile and leave their website and social media development for later down the track after they have started generating revenue.

- **A personal branding and reputation tool** – LinkedIn allows you to tell your own individual or enterprize story. You have the ability to create a LinkedIn Profile that appears in search results for your name or keywords and then deliver a user experience that encourages the right people to contact you directly. You can also add some bling – images, videos, links etc as well as invite others to provide Endorsements or Recommendations to verify your authenticity. By showing who you are connected to, visitors to your LinkedIn Profile can make additional assessments about your suitability for an opportunity. The Open to Work and Providing Services sections also help the right people find you.

- **A way for you to massage your message** – you have probably heard that 'everyone deserves a second chance.' Whilst I do not endorse the publication of any false information, I do encourage people to share information in a way that supports their goals. For example, if someone has been incarcerated for a crime and served their sentence, getting back out there into everyday life is ultimately essential and explaining what they have been doing during their incarceration in a positive way is essential. If you have had a career break or time out for illness or caring responsibilities, you can discuss other things you have learned or observed during this time (which is better than the Career Break option in my view). LinkedIn can also be used to build your online reputation and ensure that your LinkedIn Profile appears in search engine results before previous bad news reports. It may be necessary to work with an experienced LinkedIn Specialist to massage your message effectively. For example, if incarcerated, you could mention the 'holding company' as the employer whilst you were studying or completing various tasks in the detention facility.

- **A way for you to increase the size of your digital footprint** – as a well-known and reputable social media platform, LinkedIn usually always provides a link for your name on the first page of search engine result pages (provided it has been optimized and you are not up against significant competition from a person or business with the same name in the same location). It also enables you to tell the viewer of your LinkedIn Profile about the other online connections you have (via people in your network, website links, keywords in your content, recent activity, Recommendations etc).

- **A perceived reliable source of information for due diligence purposes** – as so many people are now familiar with the name 'LinkedIn,' when LinkedIn links appear in search engine results, decision-makers regularly click the LinkedIn link, especially if they are already familiar with the LinkedIn Platform. As a general rule, if the link to your LinkedIn Profile is one of the first three links in search engine results, it is also likely to be clicked. Once the person is visiting your LinkedIn Profile, they can make an assessment are review the information supplied, shared Connections, Endorsements, Recommendations, Media inclusions etc. They can then confirm or deny their perception by reaching out to Shared Connections that they already trust to discuss the authenticity of the person they are considering for work or business.

- **An international research tool** – if you are thinking about living, working or networking either at home or abroad, LinkedIn can give you direct access to leading experts worldwide. You can then reach out to them directly rather than try and find them independently or try and get past personal gate keepers (like their personal assistant or consulting advisors). In the past, senior leaders were very difficult to access. I love using a Google Advanced Search https://www.google.com.au/advanced_search so that I can search the entire LinkedIn database - I put the details of my query in the search box and choose 'LinkedIn.com' in the site box. This gives me unlimited searches on LinkedIn and includes searches beyond people in my LinkedIn network.

- **A way to generate lifetime published content** that can also go viral – quality Articles can be added to your LinkedIn Profile or LinkedIn Page and receive a Reaction (Like), Comment, Repost (Share) or Sent to others. LinkedIn Page Posts can add to your online presence and be Shared via employees and Connections. This can increase the size of your online digital footprint and content reach.

- **A career and enterprize attraction tool** – a professionally updated and active LinkedIn presence can be aligned to the career or business opportunities you want to attract so you can then deliver results. Constant adjustments have enabled me to eliminate time wasting correspondence and accelerate aligned business opportunities. My LinkedIn presence has generated international invitations and opportunities aligned with my values, strengths and context. Some of my clients have changed industries or professions and secured significant promotions and new business by adjusting their LinkedIn content and strategies, without completing further costly formal education (but sometimes some fabulous free or low cost micro credentials).

- **Look for jobs, attract jobs, showcase your services** – you can update your Career Interests on LinkedIn so that Recruiters can know that you are looking for work and LinkedIn can send you details of specific jobs you may be interested in applying for across several locations. You can select five job titles through the 'Open to Work' feature and mention on-site and remote locations. If you choose 'Providing Services' you can list up to 10 services (see Section 12.1 for more details).

- **A direct source of career and enterprize leads and overall branding** – optimizing your LinkedIn Profile and LinkedIn Pages can help you generate direct leads and sales on a regular basis. You can adjust your activity and behavior to help people understand your offering and let viewers decide for themselves if you or your enterprize are a fit. It is also a great way to share your brand story.

- **Engage in a timely and meaningful way** – when you are 'seen' on social media, people are reminded of your value offering and can appreciate and remember your supportive engagement with their content. I choose to be friendly and professional at all times, not personal, negative or confrontational. Social media and technical website professionals will remind you that you need to have an active social media presence and a website to remain relevant and appear in search engine results. Too long without any social media engagement (Reactions, Comments and Reposts) or new content (curated or created) can leave you falling behind in search engine results. However, there is no requirement to spend hours a week online. I usually suggest around 20 minutes a week on LinkedIn unless you have a specific goal. Be careful not to fall into a time wasting vortex on any social media platform. I recommend that you engage with other people's content first, publish content on your own website second and share that content on social media third. This means you have an eternal backup of content you have produced on your own website. There is no guarantee that anything you publish elsewhere will remain online (so take a copy if you wish to keep a record - even if you just copy/paste it into an email and send it to yourself with a copy of the Post link).

- **A professional development resource** – when you select the right Influencers to follow, Connections to add, Groups to join, Companies to follow, items to React (Like), Comment or Repost (Share) to, your Newsfeed and Notifications will constantly provide relevant information and inspiration for your own professional development. You can choose to hide irrelevant updates (click on the three dots on the top right hand side of a Post) and you can unsubscribe from Groups, Companies, Newsletters and Hashtags if the information provided is no longer aligned with your goals. If you are connected to people you really like, click the Notification Bell on their LinkedIn Profile and/or Page to receive most of their Post Notifications.

- **A timely way for you to generate the user experience you want** – if you find that LinkedIn is generating too many emails, enquiries or Connection requests, you can simply modify your content, signals, and Communication Settings https://www.linkedin.com/psettings/communications to generate the experience you want. It may take a few moments to change these settings but it can save you from having your email inbox overloaded (and your view of LinkedIn tarnished). Your alternative option is to set up a rule on your email inbox to put all emails from LinkedIn.com into a separate folder.

- **Build your enterprize presence online** – through your employees, stakeholders, network connections, backlinks, Articles, Events, Groups and more. A platform that has such a significant database, constantly updated algorithms and the ability to implement your own strategic signals process is worth optimizing.

As mentioned earlier, this book will help you complete your LinkedIn Profile and teach you how to use LinkedIn to develop your network, maintain those relationships with semi-frequent activity, attract aligned individuals and opportunities and achieve your career and business goals both now and in the future. At all times, it will focus on ethical and respectful practice.

2.2 LinkedIn Hang Ups

It is fair to say that I have heard a lot of objections about LinkedIn over the years. As with any technological offering, there are pluses and minuses and any technology based solution will never be 100% perfect. If you can use it to 80% of its capacity, you will achieve amazing results.

I believe that LinkedIn is like the 'goose that lays golden eggs' (from the Aesop fable). If we all look after LinkedIn and treat it respectfully, then we all have the chance to keep receiving those golden eggs. But if we try and create automated or coercive shortcuts, we run the risk of killing the goose and then everyone will miss out on the golden eggs.

Unfortunately, due to some people's bad behavior on LinkedIn, some privileges that have been enjoyed in the past have been removed to prevent spamming, inappropriate connection or sales requests and even unwanted dating proposals! LinkedIn has to constantly adjust the internal algorithm and user options to detect and prevent inappropriate behavior on LinkedIn.

When you visit a LinkedIn Profile, you can choose the 'More' button and 'About this profile' and it will show you what year the person joined, how recently they have updated their information and if their contact details have been verified. If you view a LinkedIn Profile and believe it is suspicious, please take a moment to report it.

Despite the bad behavior that has to be monitored, from a user perspective, the most common hang ups about LinkedIn I hear include:

- **No privacy** – my response is that it is your past history and you need to have an online digital footprint so that you can be found and verified online (however, if you have personal security issues or are working in a classified confidential role, there are settings you can adjust for this purpose or you may need to Hibernate your Profile). Please do not include your date of birth on the platform (check here https://www.linkedin.com/in/YOURURL/edit/forms/contact-info/new/).

- **Don't know who to connect to** – this depends on your values, strengths and context and it is perfectly okay to decline an invitation request and the person sending the invite will not be sent a message saying you declined their invitation. You need to create your own 'LinkedIn Connection Policy' and then you can easily decide whether to say yes or no when a request is received.

- **Too much time to fill it in or add content** – once the content has been added, you only need to tweak it later. If adding valuable content helps you attract a relevant opportunity, maintain your network and/or make sales, then it is a very worthwhile investment of your time and energy. It also saves you a lot of time explaining your past or even trying to remember your past, especially the dates!

- **Too costly** – most features mentioned in this book are available via the free LinkedIn Profile.

- **Scared of computers** – in modern society, we need to show our digital competency (application of technology), not just our digital literacy (use of technology and creation of a LinkedIn Profile).

- **Don't know what my employer allows** – you can read and understand their Social Media Policy or guidelines first.

- **Too many emails** – you can update the frequency of Email Communications to daily or weekly digests or turn them off at https://www.linkedin.com/psettings/communications-controls/email. You can also set up a rule in your email inbox to place all emails from LinkedIn.com in the one folder and you can check all email messages from LinkedIn in the one place (and not be distracted throughout your workday). I have turned off email notifications for new Connection requests and just deal with these when I logon to LinkedIn.

- **It seems overwhelming and I am a very private person** – try updating your LinkedIn Profile with a friend or pay for some expert assistance from a LinkedIn Specialist, Career Specialist or Social Media Professional who uses LinkedIn ethically and effectively in your niche and whom you can relate to on a personal level. Ideally, they would have some lived experience or connections in your industry or profession to be able to optimize it for your purpose.

- **Too much spam** – LinkedIn is constantly updating their security protocols to prevent the creation of a fake Profile or false employment records (saying you work for XYZ when you don't). They have excellent detection tools that identify annoying or inappropriate behavior and they will suspend or remove LinkedIn Profiles without warning. I always recommend reporting bad behavior so that it can be checked immediately and prevent other users from having a bad experience on LinkedIn.

I understand that LinkedIn is not necessarily the favorite social media platform for people who are getting the results they would like on other social media platforms or through other channels.

I still believe it is an essential part of your social media mix, because it helps you build your network and at the end of the day, success in your career or business depends on the quality of your relationships, not just your present level of income or sales you are generating via another social media platform. If you choose to retire, you will still need a network that you can reconnect with at the level that works for you and you may also wish to share different news in the future (e.g. voluntary work).

I also believe that the ability to build and maintain an international network makes LinkedIn a key component of your career or business strategy, regardless of how you currently secure career or business opportunities. It also saves you a lot of time as your network members update their own details and you can reach out to them at any time!

If you add people to an email list and they change their email address, you can lose contact. If they are on LinkedIn and you are connected, you can visit their LinkedIn Profile to see their current email address or send them a message via LinkedIn and see if it has been read and see the history of your conversation as well.

In fact I make it a policy of inviting everyone who joins my mailing lists or registers for my events to invite them to connect with me on LinkedIn. I also invite everyone I meet personally or professionally to connect with me on LinkedIn (although I don't recommend connecting with patients if you are in a medical role). You may also like to invite people you meet throughout your job search process, whilst studying or prospecting for sales.

2.3 Make Sure You Only Have One LinkedIn Profile

I have worked with some clients who have up to four separate LinkedIn Profiles when they come to see me. This happens because they usually create a Profile with one email address and then accidentally open another Profile with a different email address because they couldn't remember the password (you cannot use the same email address on multiple LinkedIn Profiles). They may also do this because they no longer have access to the original email address and can't work out how to re-issue a password without access to an email address.

For this reason, I recommend that you add all of your current and past email addresses to one LinkedIn Profile at https://www.linkedin.com/psettings/email even if you no longer have access to the previous email address. This means that anyone reaching out to you via your previous email address can 'find you' on LinkedIn and they will be redirected to the one LinkedIn Profile and you will not accidentally create a duplicate LinkedIn Profile with one of your many email addresses.

You may also choose to add your phone number to your LinkedIn Profile at https://www.linkedin.com/psettings/phone so that you can have two factor authentication when you sign in or use your phone number to login if you lose access to your email address. If you do not want to use your phone number for two factor authentication, you can use an Authenticator App instead.

If you lose access to your email address and you didn't provide LinkedIn with your phone number, you can still 'identify' yourself with LinkedIn by sending them some photo identification and a new email address and after they verify your information, they will re-instate your access. This may take a few days but it means you can re-gain entry to a previously established LinkedIn Profile.

If you are not careful when you create a LinkedIn Profile, you will authorize LinkedIn to go through your email address contacts and/or your mobile phone contacts and LinkedIn will invite these people to connect with you on LinkedIn. This sounds convenient at the time until you realize that old girlfriends, boyfriends, annoying workmates and Great Aunty Bertha are all invited to connect with you on LinkedIn. It is called syncing.

If you turn on this syncing authorization by mistake, you can turn it off at https://www.linkedin.com/mynetwork/settings/manage-syncing.

If you are in the unfortunate position of having multiple LinkedIn Profiles, you can merge them at https://www.linkedin.com/psettings/account-preferences (once you have re-gained password access).

Ideally, you would keep the 'oldest' LinkedIn Profile and merge the newer one/s, but it is vital that you backup your data before you do this (by Saving your Profile to PDF and Getting a Copy of Your Data which may take a few days) and that you ensure you have password access to each Profile so that you can complete the merge process on the first attempt.

Remember, the information on the LinkedIn Profiles will not be merged (only the Connections) so make sure you have kept a copy of any messages, invitation requests and LinkedIn Profile content that is important from the Profile that is 'closing.' If you have the full backups available and find that you accidentally merged the Profiles the wrong way around, you can still find the information you had on the other LinkedIn Profile via the backup data.

Ideally you will login to the LinkedIn Profile with the most information (hopefully also the one you opened first) and then merge with the Profile with less information.

Even if you have multiple 'personalities' in your working life (for example, I am an Independent LinkedIn Specialist and I also write poetry which is unrelated), you still only need one LinkedIn Profile. You just need to decide which personality is most important for attracting opportunities and focus the priority keywords in the most important LinkedIn Profile locations (for example, the Headline, About section and Job Titles).

I know one person who has two LinkedIn Profiles in different names. One LinkedIn Profile uses a pseudonym name that is different to his real name because he writes erotic fiction. His other LinkedIn Profile is in his real name because he has a 'day job' writing government policy. He also had to declare his erotic fiction role to his employer.

If you use the same name for two different LinkedIn Profiles (for example, one where you are an Accountant and the other a Photographer), you run the risk of people accidentally connecting to the wrong LinkedIn Profile and it is way too confusing to try and make people connect with the 'right' person with the same name on LinkedIn. Remember, one name, one person, one LinkedIn Profile.

Alternatively, you could consider sharing your separate content via two different LinkedIn Pages but still having only one LinkedIn Profile for your name. For example, I could have one LinkedIn Page called 'Sue Ellson LinkedIn Specialist' and one called 'Sue Ellson Author.' At this stage, I have one LinkedIn Profile and one LinkedIn Page and they are both called Sue Ellson.

Don't forget, you will only ever be one person even if you do have multiple personalities or work types and as the world of work changes, I am sure many people will have more than one main skill set or enterprize offering and I already know that LinkedIn are adjusting around this Skills focus in the future.

You might say that you do polywork, or are a 'slashy' (do lots of different types of work), a gigster, a multipotentialite or even have a portfolio career. LinkedIn gives you the space to record all of these offerings and the only thing you need to decide is the order in which they are listed (and you can choose by income, preference or passion).

Also, please make sure that if you are using a forward slash / or pipe | between words in any of your content on LinkedIn that you put a space either side of the slash or pipe. If you don't, a search query will see Owner/Operator as one word OwnerOperator which means you will not be found for either Owner or Operator.

3. Before Starting On LinkedIn

Whether you are about to create a LinkedIn Profile or you already have a LinkedIn Profile, this book will be most helpful if you think about what you are planning to achieve in the short, medium and long term.

How can you attract the right opportunities if you are not sharing the right message with the right keywords in the right locations?

As a Career Specialist, I can assure you that there are many different ways to decide how you would like to move forward in your career, work, business or enterprize journey.

Some years ago, I spent three years reading various books on how to choose your career and even after all of that self-education and reflection, I still didn't have an answer. I ended up developing my own values-aligned decision-making framework.

The process began with understanding that in the modern world, we have so many choices available to us. The only way to reduce this range of options is to create your own values-aligned decision-making framework so that when an opportunity appears, you can pass it through your personal framework to help you make a values-aligned decision. Let me assure you, it saves you from 'shiny object syndrome' and helps keep you focused on your goals, not someone else's persuasion techniques.

3.1 Decision-Making Framework – Values, Strengths, Context

I would like to encourage you to think about three things.

Firstly, your **values**. What are your most important values? Is an immediate income your primary value right now? Perhaps you would like to follow a dream or fulfil a purpose. Perhaps finding the right employer with the right workplace culture is important to you. Perhaps you have a side hustle that you want to take to the next level. Perhaps you already have a business but it is time to systemize your operations.

Take a moment to write down some of your highest values. If you are not sure where to start, think about how you currently spend most of your time, what you think about most frequently, what you talk about the most or where you spend most of your money. Alternatively, think about what you wanted to do when you finished secondary school and also, what your primary caregivers, family and friends have done (as you will have learnt a lot of skills by osmosis by being around these people).

Also think about the value you offer - your personality, your ethics, your approach. What will other people find valuable?

My Values – Yours and Others

____

____

____

Secondly, your **strengths**. This includes both natural strengths (what feels like a natural talent and is easy for you to do) and acquired strengths (what you have learnt as a skill and enjoy doing). You may have some natural strengths that you don't like doing and some learned strengths that you love doing.

For example, I am good at accounting but I don't like doing it. I learned how to use LinkedIn effectively and I love using it and educating others about it.

Remember that some strengths are best kept for 'hobby' mode rather than work or enterprize mode if you have a high value of earning an income right now and that current strength does not generate an adequate income yet. You may also like to record some weaknesses as either areas to build on in the future or to avoid completely (I refuse to do any work related to gambling or horse racing).

My Strengths – Natural and Acquired

____

____

____

Thirdly, your **context**. This is about what is happening in your life right now. Your personal circumstances and commitments, perhaps even your current health, wealth, intellectual or emotional challenges that affect your ability to make certain choices. For example, if you have young children and unreliable childcare options, this may limit your ability to secure a full time job with a lengthy commute so your priority may be a work-from-home opportunity right now.

My Context – Circumstances and Commitments

____

____

____

Once you know your values, strengths and context, you can then choose how to use LinkedIn more effectively. Of course if any of these change over time, you can simply adjust your LinkedIn Profile again. That is the joy of online content, it is only ever a version number and it can be changed at any time. Before you make any changes, save a copy of your Profile to PDF. After you make the changes, save a copy again.

3.2 Choosing Your Career Or Business

Whilst looking at your Values, Strengths and Context may be enough to determine your future direction for now, for other people, a bit more guided reflection and processing is required.

One way to start is by simply completing your LinkedIn Profile with all of the information you have up until today (even if you are only 16 and still in secondary school). If you choose to work with a Career Specialist, preparing the first draft in your own time is a fantastic first step as it gives them a good background on what you have done so far and a lot of information you can discuss, particularly if you go into detail with your tasks and achievements or impacts.

However, to build on from the first step of identifying your Values, Strengths and Context, the next stage is to explore this more visually with a Mind Map. Here's what I did with my Mind Map in my late 20's. It has served me ever since because it created my very own values-aligned decision-making framework.

1. Review

In the middle of the page, I drew a circle and wrote down my absolute non-negotiables. The items that no matter what, were essential to my new life. They were modest and realistic and focused on the location, work-style, learning-style, income-style and future life-style.

I then started looking back over my working life at ALL of the things I had done and started writing them down by drawing branches off the sides of the circle.

As my career started in banking, I drew a circle at the end of the branch and expanded on the many different things I had done at the bank.

I followed this up with other branches and circles related to my other voluntary roles and activities outside of work.

2. Reflect

I then started to record all of the things I had always thought would be interesting to do, without evaluation or censorship via new branches and circles. There were some wild and crazy ideas as well as sensible and logical ideas. If they came to mind, I wrote them down.

I did this until I exhausted all of the ideas in my head and heart. This is a private process for you to do and you do not need to show it to anyone else unless you would like to.

3. Recalibrate

It was now time to put the Mind Map aside until the next day and come back with a colored pen, pencil or marker and circle the items that really resonated with me.

This was a really exciting process as it showed me what I truly valued and it gave me a values-aligned decision-making framework that was right for me.

It helped me create a template that could be used to assess any opportunity that appeared in the future.

4. Record

The next step was the most time consuming. I added everything that was relevant to my résumé (and later my LinkedIn Profile) so that I could showcase the most aligned achievements and tasks using as many keywords as possible that related to the work I was interested in completing.

It felt good to leave out the items that didn't reflect my new focus and it felt even better to discuss the highlights of my career so far. This process really gave me clarity as no-one knows me better than I know myself.

I also noticed that some of the items I listed were related to the tasks within a role and others were related to the people I worked with. This highlighted that I needed a combination of tasks and people in my future. I am sure everyone can relate to the joy of working with people they like and also completing tasks that they like versus the opposite.

It also helped me reflect on the location of the work I had completed. I really enjoyed working close to home and feeling more connected to my local community.

5. Research

With this new-found clarity, I started asking various people questions and tweaked my content and started building intentional networks. I asked several different people about the options available to me. I had to make sure that the advice I received didn't have a hidden agenda or any form of bias. I also needed to make sure that there was genuine demand for the type of work I was interested in doing and balance that commitment with my personal life.

I will never forget talking to one woman in particular. We met for coffee and she told me she had 'given up' her career to raise her young children as a stay-at-home mother. Whilst she did not regret the time she had spent with her children, she was very aware that the time out of the workforce had a negative impact on her career. She didn't suggest not having children or working full time, she simply emphasized that it was important to maintain a professional identity and skills throughout that phase of life.

With this new information, I updated my résumé and attended relevant events with people in the industries of interest. I wasn't sure if it would work or not, but with a clear intention, all sorts of opportunities started coming my way.

6. Respond

Now it was time to decide what I would do next. I was fortunate to attract a range of offers almost immediately and I evaluated each one according to my non-negotiables and values criteria from the Mind Map exercise.

It was exciting to say no to the opportunities that weren't aligned and know that each time I said no, I was getting closer to my dream work. That said, I did ensure that I was still earning enough money to pay the bills and I kept my savings intact. I did some 'work for now' (also known as a 'job for now') to tide me over. This is why understanding your context is so important.

7. Restart

Once I had gone through the research and decision phase, it was time to restart and put all of my energy into my future direction. What I like most about this career direction process was that I created my own options. I didn't need someone else to 'tell me what to do.' I simply created a process to follow that allowed me to work out what was right for me, with relevant input and advice from others.

The alternative is to organize a professional appointment with an independent Career Specialist (not somebody who works in a training organization and suggests you complete a new course). Career Specialists often use additional tools, assessments and processes and ideally, if they have good referral networks, they can save you a lot of time and effort and introduce options that you may not have even known about. If they have networks of contacts in your areas of interest, even better.

In the end, a traditional 'career' wasn't the right option for me, my own enterprize was! How surprising. With a society and a family that had always encouraged me to find a job, the idea that I could do a variety of work and be living a more aligned life was both exciting and a bit terrifying. A lot of people disagreed with my choice. In fact, they still do despite the fact I have been doing it for over 20 years!

I am not recommending this option if you are not fully ready to take on this high level of risk because it is not for the faint-hearted. As a result of going from corporate to self-employment, I wrote the book 'Gigsters - Any Age or Ability Employees, Experts and Entrepreneurs' to help other people who are considering work rather than a job.

I define a Gigster as someone who uses technology to attract aligned gigs. The book includes specific tips on how to go about it, with a particular emphasis on money management (think assets and wealth rather than pay and benefits) and the joy of being your own kind of peculiar.

The above values-aligned decision-making framework and seven step career direction process is designed to help you select and seek the work (career or business) that is right for you.

I hope you find it useful. I have shared it with many career clients over the years and it has helped people attract a wide range of incredible opportunities, particularly those seeking an aligned life.

What is especially interesting is that even now, so many years later, my original Mind Map is still providing me with a values-aligned decision-making framework. That is because my own values are constant and not based on any career or business. It has allowed me to truly be me in all aspects of my life.

3.3 Setup, Shine, Surprise Methodology

Once you are clear on your Values, Strengths and Context and have your own values-aligned decision-making framework and you have chosen the most relevant career or business for now or the near future, it is time to implement your own LinkedIn Strategy that supports your values, purpose, goals and objectives.

In many cultures and faiths, there is a belief around 'ask and you will receive.' However, it is very hard to receive if the 'provider' does not know what you want.

I have found that some clients, despite all of my strategies for clarifying their future direction, still feel stuck. This could be for many different reasons and despite the discomfort they feel, I encourage them to press on with completing their LinkedIn Profile.

You may be surprised by this suggestion. Surely you cannot head towards a destination without knowing how to get there?

I believe that we sometimes find the destination we are seeking after taking a few steps forward. If you are over the age of 16, you will have some experience, even if that is only in the area of education and training. Your parents or caregivers gave you insights into their career or business. Your friends, family and fellow students have shared stories with you too.

If you decide to complete your LinkedIn Profile up to today's date, you will be able to reflect on everything you have done up to this point. The items you enjoyed more or less. The people who were aligned or not aligned. The activities that matched your values and abilities. The enterprizes and individuals that inspired you. The locations that suit you best.

Here are the steps in my Setup, Shine, Surprise Methodology. This is simply a broad picture overview.

The Setup Steps are there to remind you of what everyone must do to gain value from LinkedIn.

The Shine Steps are there to ensure you stay focused on your values, purpose, goals and objectives.

The Surprise Steps are there to finesse your activity in a 'courageous character' way.

Setup Steps

1. Backup Your Profile and Collect your Statistics (Section 4.2 and 4.3)

2. Change your Settings (Section 5)

3. Complete your LinkedIn Profile (Section 7) and Page (Section 8)

Shine Steps

4. Engage (Section 10)

5. Curate and/or Create (Section 11)

6. Collaborate (Section 11.6)

Surprise Steps

7. Review (Section 14)

8. Revise (Section 14)

9. Implement new features (Section 14)

[illegible]

[illegible]

[illegible]

[illegible]

[illegible]

[illegible]

Set-up Steps

1. [illegible]

2. [illegible]

3. Complete your LinkedIn [illegible] Section 7 and 8 [illegible]

Bonus Steps

1. Enhance Section 10 [illegible]

2. Community [illegible] (Section 11)

3. [illegible] (Section 12)

Surprise Steps

1. [illegible] Section 14

2. [illegible] (Section 15)

3. Implement new features (Section 16)

4. Starting On LinkedIn

Ideally, you will logon to LinkedIn via a laptop or desktop computer and have your mobile device (phone) handy as well.

4.1 Why You Need To Complete Your Own LinkedIn Profile

I cannot overstate the importance of **COMPLETING YOUR OWN LINKEDIN PROFILE**. Yes you! I want to make reading this book worthwhile for you!!

Some of my clients and students have been reluctant to put their details online, but the reality is that most decision-makers will search for online content about you before meeting you online or in person, so you need to be findable and verifiable.

The best word of mouth referral could be worth nothing if the person receiving that referral cannot verify your details. If they can't find you online, they may never contact you at all. People without an online presence can sometimes be considered suspicious or out-of-date.

Please let me remind you that you only need to publish what feels comfortable for you. I insist that it be honest but it can be massaged to read better and focus on the best and most relevant aspects of your story.

If you tell your story adequately, you only need to tell your story once! If you feel awkward talking about yourself, ask for some help. A lot of my clients tell me that they find it easier to write about someone else rather than about themselves. If this applies to you, try working with someone to produce your content or work on an exchange basis with someone else.

In my view, we lost our privacy in the 20th century – as soon as our information started going online. Now that we live in an online world, keeping a **record of our achievements or impacts** and tasks online is valuable for a variety of reasons. Firstly, five years from now we are likely to forget most of what we are doing today, especially with the current rate of technological change.

Secondly, once our story is online, we don't have to keep repeating it over and over again to each new person we meet. It can be a **handy reference point and validation tool**. This is very helpful for people who have made a significant career shift and those nosy people wanting to know how you got to your current role or whether they should value your contribution at work. Yes, even people at parties have been known to check you out online before talking to you in detail. Parents often check out details of their child's school teacher.

Thirdly, it helps you **attract opportunities**. All of this information on your LinkedIn Profile can be filled with keywords that search queries can use to identify your value and help you appear in relevant search results.

For example, at the very beginning of my career, I helped discover fraudulent banking transactions. Many years later, a recruiter contacted me for a role associated with finding and preventing fraudulent behavior via my LinkedIn Profile. The word 'fraud' was written once in my LinkedIn Profile from a role that I finished many years prior, but it was enough to help me be found, contacted and asked to apply for the role.

Remember that LinkedIn is essentially a huge database and if you don't put the words in, you won't be found in a search query for those words. I often say that if you 'don't tell, you can't sell.' This is very different to the past where you wouldn't reveal any information to a prospect until you had the sale.

For you to gain maximum value from this book, please **COMPLETE YOUR LinkedIn PROFILE based on the suggestions that are relevant for you** – even if you are working for someone else and don't plan to change your job anytime soon.

I am here to help make completing your LinkedIn Profile and using it for your goals as simple and effective as possible. You will be able to see the results of your efforts by seeing how your statistics change.

If you consider yourself to be 'retired,' I would still recommend that you keep your LinkedIn Profile. You can mention, "Only interested in reconnecting with former colleagues or answering family tree enquiries." Think how valuable you can be to someone doing family tree research if you can be found! Likewise, if you are now involved in voluntary community projects, you can use LinkedIn to encourage others to get involved or to showcase the success of the voluntary projects. Whilst many new retirees spend the first few years unwinding, at some point, many people like to reconnect with former peers, colleagues and friends.

Despite how the LinkedIn Newsfeed appears to have a lot of content, most people on LinkedIn do not produce content, they just read and scan and do not engage or add a Reaction (Like) or a Comment or Repost (Share) or Send it to others. They may dwell on the content, actually pause whilst scrolling and read it (this activity is called dwell time and is an important metric for LinkedIn to decide if the content is actually interesting and helps determine if it will be circulated more widely).

If you are not sure where to start with the LinkedIn Newsfeed, I encourage you engage first (React (Like) and/or Comment) and in the future, either curate (share) other people's content or create your own content.

4.2 Before You Start, Backup Your LinkedIn Data First

I would like to encourage you to take a backup of your LinkedIn Profile before you start modifying it and I would like to encourage you to take regular backups of your LinkedIn data from now on. There are two main ways to do this.

1. **Save your LinkedIn Profile content to a PDF** every time before and after you update your LinkedIn Profile. You can do this via the More button on your own LinkedIn Profile. Make sure your internet browser settings are changed to 'Ask where to save files before downloading' so that you can save your file with today's date back to front, your name and 'LinkedIn Profile' in the file name e.g. YYYY-MM-DD-sue-ellson-LinkedIn-profile.pdf. This makes it easy to identify when you last completed this task just by looking at the file name. You can also visit anyone else's LinkedIn Profile and save it to PDF as well and 'borrow ideas' for use in your LinkedIn Profile. Please don't print out a LinkedIn Profile on paper unless absolutely necessary - for example, you would need a lot of paper to print out my LinkedIn Profile!

2. By manually **requesting a copy of your LinkedIn data** in the settings https://www.linkedin.com/psettings/member-data. LinkedIn will send you an email with a link and you need to download the files immediately. I recommend that you do this at least every six months. In the unlikely event that your LinkedIn Profile is lost or deleted, this way you will have some record of your online network. Look for the file called 'Inferences about you.' This explains what LinkedIn has inferred about you based on your profile and activity on LinkedIn and can make interesting reading.

4.3 Your Current LinkedIn Statistics And Goals

To find out whether or not the edits you make to your LinkedIn Profile after reading this book are worthwhile, you will need to write down your real-time statistics now so that you have a reference point to come back to later on. Appendix B at the back of the book provides a summary.

The following list allows you to record specific numbers and details and provides my recommendations as to the minimum numbers you should have for each one. They all include a direct link on where to find the number on LinkedIn (this link may change in the future). Over time, you will remember where to find these statistics without clicking on the links.

If you write these numbers down now as 'point in time figures', complete the suggestions in this book and then compare them in three months from now, you will be able to see how your statistics have improved after editing your LinkedIn Profile (please, please, please update your LinkedIn Profile as you read this book).

The seven items marked with an *asterisk are the most important baseline statistics I would encourage you to collect.

Today's Date: ___/___/___

1. **Number of Connections*** – people you are connected to.
   (Maximum of 30,000, Minimum 60+, Over time 500+)
   https://www.linkedin.com/mynetwork
   Number_____

2. **Number of Followers*** – people who follow your content, may or may not be connected to you.
   (Maximum unlimited, suggest you aim for more Followers than Connections as a significantly higher number of Followers suggests you could be a thought leader or influencer).
   https://www.linkedin.com/feed/followers
   Number _____

3. **Number you are Following** – people whose content you follow, may or may not be connected to you and includes People, and Pages etc
   (Maximum unlimited, suggest you be selective about how many different types of Pages you follow and consider following Companies that you would like to engage with in the future).
   https://www.linkedin.com/feed/followers
   Number _____

4. **Profile Views last 90 days*** – This reflects the number of people who have actually looked at some or all of your LinkedIn Profile. I like to click on this link and see who has looked at me (I call this 'reverse stalking'). I find it very informative and it is my favorite thing to do on LinkedIn because it tells me whether or not my LinkedIn Profile is attracting the people who can benefit from my offerings. If I recognize people who have contacted me, I am super excited that they have checked me out beforehand. Likewise, if my clients look at me after our appointment, I am optimistic that they are completing their follow up tasks. In your case, these people could all be classified as warm leads and may be worth contacting directly.
   (Aim for 100+ per 90 days and more over time)
   https://www.linkedin.com/me/profile-views
   Number _____

5. **Views of your Posts or Articles*** – this will vary every time you publish a Post or Article on LinkedIn. Securing 1,000+ views for a Post and 100+ views for an Article within the first few days of publication is a very good starting point. However, this statistic will depend on the quality of the item and the engagement that occurs during that time. It is a good idea to create content that has a high dwell time which means that people stop scrolling and keep

looking at your content. The more interesting and engaging the content, the better!
https://www.linkedin.com/analytics/creator/?resultType=IMPRESSIONS&timeRange=past_7_days
Impressions past 7 Days ______

6. **Search Appearances last 7 days*** – this helps you understand if your LinkedIn Profile is sourcing its own LinkedIn search traffic, without you being popular for a particular Post, job application or other publicity (which would show as a high number of Profile Viewers but not necessarily a high number of Search Appearances).
   (Aim for 50+ per 7 days and more over time)
   https://www.linkedin.com/me/search-appearances
   Number ______

7. **Number of Featured Skills and Endorsements*** – you can have up to 50 Skills listed on your LinkedIn Profile. Aim to have at least 20 votes for each of the top three 'pinned' skills and ensure that the top three are most related to the type of career or business you are seeking.
   Your own LinkedIn Profile page
   e.g. https://www.linkedin.com/in/YOURURL
   Skill 1 ____ Votes _____

   Skill 2 ____ Votes _____

   Skill 3 ____ Votes _____

8. **Number of Recommendations*** – you can both give and receive Recommendations to and from your Connections. I encourage you to have at least six that you have given and six that you have received.
   Your own LinkedIn Profile page
   e.g. https://www.linkedin.com/in/YOURURL

   Received ____

   Given ____

9. **Number of Reactions (Likes)** – engaging with other people's content helps the algorithm understand that you 'listen' as well as 'speak' and increases your Engagement Ratio and your 'Personal Encourager' status. Recommend three or more per week.
   https://www.linkedin.com/in/YOURURL/recent-activity/
   Reactions ____ last week

10. **Number of Comments** – recommend one or more per week and write as much as possible whilst still remaining relevant to the content of the Post or Article, ideally using keywords that are in

the Post or Article.
https://www.linkedin.com/in/YOURURL/recent-activity
Comments ___ last week

11. **Number of Posts** – this relates to the content you add into the Newsfeed and if you are actively using LinkedIn for a specific goal, I would recommend posting once a week. If not actively using LinkedIn, I would suggest one Post per month. This includes content that you have curated, created or co-created.
https://www.linkedin.com/in/YOURURL/detail/recent-activity/shares
Posts ___ last month

12. **Number of Articles** – this relates to the content you add as an Article that stays on LinkedIn indefinitely. If you are actively using LinkedIn for a specific goal, I would recommend posting once a month. If not actively using LinkedIn, I would suggest one every three or four months (three or four times a year). This does not include Newsletters.
https://www.linkedin.com/in/YOURURL/detail/recent-activity/posts
Articles ___ last three months

13. **Number of Groups** – joining groups helps LinkedIn understand your priorities and interests. I do not have a recommended number, but it is a good idea to look for groups with high levels of engagement and good moderators.
https://www.linkedin.com/groups/
Group Participation ___ times in the last month

14. **Number of Schools or Universities** – if you have studied at a particular school or university or are a member of a well-recognized professional association that has a School Page on LinkedIn, it is a good idea, even if you did not complete your studies with the Education Provider, to list this in the Education section of your LinkedIn Profile.

    This will then add you to their alumni and help other alumni find you in their LinkedIn search results. It will also give you a lead into other countries and industries to connect with someone else who has studied at the same School if you visit the School Page and search through the Alumni feature. If you only completed part of a course, you can mention 'Subjects Completed' rather than saying you were a 'dropout' or not including that part of your Education on your LinkedIn Profile. If you have some relevant Topics that were covered in your studies, you can mention 'Topics Included'. If you finished a course, you can mention your Conferral date. https://www.linkedin.com/in/YOURURL/edit/education/new/

15. **Social Selling Index** – this ranks you and your LinkedIn activity in comparison to your industry and the people in your network and can be found online at https://www.linkedin.com/sales/ssi. Technically, the closer you are to the top 1%, the 'better.' I believe that the SSI score is most relevant for people using LinkedIn for Social Selling and if you are securing the results you would like, I would not be monitoring this as a key metric. It is related to the LinkedIn Sales Navigator product.

16. **My Network Dashboard** – available at https://www.linkedin.com/mynetwork on the left menu, this lists your Number of Connections, Teammates (people you have identified as colleagues – you can add up to one manager, 19 teammates who report to your manager, 20 direct reports, and 30 other teammates and it is only visible to you but helps tailor your Newsfeed and Notifications), Contacts (people you have imported in to the LinkedIn Platform from your phone or email account that you synced with LinkedIn), People I Follow, Groups (joined), Events (attended), Pages (follow), Newsletters (subscribed) and Hashtags (follow). These figures are all very personal to you and your goals but you may like to keep a point in time record.
    Connections ____ (constantly increasing)
    Contacts ____ (constantly increasing)
    Following and followers ____ (aligned)
    Groups ____ (aligned)
    Events ____ (aligned)
    Pages ____ (aligned)
    Newsletters ____ (aligned)
    Hashtags ____ (aligned)

    When you look at these numbers, ask yourself if you are making use of these existing resources effectively. Most marketers will always suggest that the best business comes from referrals, so rather than chasing new people for sales, try reaching out to your existing Connections first.

    Alternatively, follow up all of your previous leads (it can take seven exchanges or more to secure a commitment. Ideally, if the purchaser says 'yes' at least three times during your negotiation, you are much more likely to secure a sale).

    You may like to look at who you are Connected to and Following and Endorse them for a few Skills listed on their LinkedIn Profile and write them an honest and informative Recommendation or just engage with their content.

    Are you an active participant in Groups or are you just there to let LinkedIn know that the topic is of interest to you?

    How many Events have you engaged with in the last six months?

Is now the time to register for something new? Is it worth looking at the people who attended an event that you attended and reaching out to them?

The Pages you are Following could be mostly automatic (past work Experience or Education) but also random Pages you agreed to Follow when you were invited to but they may not make any sense to keep following now, particularly if you have had a change of career, industry or profession. These could potentially be removed from your list by 'Unfollowing.'

You may be subscribed to Newsletters that are no longer relevant or you may even decide to create your own Newsletter. If you do create a Newsletter, (from the Write an Article Screen https://www.linkedin.com/post/new), it can 'invite all your Connections or Followers to subscribe. Also, after publishing each Newsletter Article, push, in-app, and email notifications are sent to all your subscribers to help drive views and you'll get real-time feedback and comments from your readers. You can understand how your content is doing with Newsletter analytics and invite Subscribers to Connect.

Hashtags are great for choosing topics of interest to you but also for tracking how well the hashtags you use are performing.

17. **Hashtags you are Following** – usually recommend less than 20 but if you are a Creator and have chosen five hashtags to talk about, you may also want to include these.
    Name of Hashtag ________________
    Name of Hashtag ________________
    Name of Hashtag ________________
    Name of Hashtag ________________
    Name of Hashtag ________________
    Name of Hashtag ________________
    Name of Hashtag ________________
    Name of Hashtag ________________
    Name of Hashtag ________________
    Name of Hashtag ________________

18. **Pages you Follow** – usually recommend that you follow all of the Companies or Schools where you would like to work or support their activity.
    https://www.linkedin.com/feed/following/?filterType=company
    Pages _____

19. **Influencers, Companies and Hashtags Following** – You can look for new Influencers, Companies and Hashtags to follow at https://www.linkedin.com/feed/follow.

The Influencers have a blue LinkedIn chat box icon next to

their name and these people have been personally selected and approved by LinkedIn to share their insights online. This link will also show you their Follower Count.

You can also sort who you are Following by the sort drop-down box on the right hand side according to

All https://www.linkedin.com/feed/following/
Connections https://www.linkedin.com/feed/following/?filterType=connection
Out of Network https://www.linkedin.com/feed/following/?filterType=member
Companies https://www.linkedin.com/feed/following/?filterType=company
Hashtags https://www.linkedin.com/feed/following/?filterType=channel

Now could be a good time to review some of these choices but also to re-engage with others.

20. **Newsletter Subscriptions** – review your list and see if you want to remain on the mailing list. Usually recommend your top 50. https://www.linkedin.com/mynetwork/network-manager/newsletters/
Name of Newsletter ______________________________
Name of Newsletter ______________________________
Name of Newsletter ______________________________
Name of Newsletter ______________________________
Name of Newsletter ______________________________
Name of Newsletter ______________________________
Name of Newsletter ______________________________
Name of Newsletter ______________________________
Name of Newsletter ______________________________
Name of Newsletter ______________________________

5. Priority Settings On Your LinkedIn Profile

Now that you have saved your LinkedIn Profile to PDF and you are waiting for your full data archive link to come through via email from LinkedIn (click the link and download the files immediately when the email does arrive because the live link is only available for 72 hours) and you have collected your LinkedIn statistics, it is now time to adjust the most important settings on your LinkedIn Profile.

I am not going to go through every individual setting here as the options do change quite frequently, but I am going to focus on the settings that provide you with strategic support for your career or business with a relevant rationale to describe 'why' it may be helpful to you.

I recommend that you go through ALL of the options at https://www.linkedin.com/psettings every six months because some options may be automatically turned on or off when the LinkedIn Platform is updated without you being notified directly.

I encourage you to choose the preferences that work for you.

5.1 Your LinkedIn Profile URL

This is where people find your LinkedIn Profile on LinkedIn. Mine is at https://www.linkedin.com/in/sueellson. You need to change it from the one that is automatically provided which looks something like "https://www.linkedin.com/in/sue-ellson-4abg7d" to the best version of your first name and last name without too much extra information.

I have been able to secure "sueellson" and this is the most favorable option. If this wasn't available, I could have used a dash (not an underscore) between my first and last name "sue-ellson." If that wasn't available, I could put pre-nominals before my name "ms-sue-ellson" or post nominals afterwards "sue-ellson-bbus" or a number "sueellson8." I do not recommend any number related to your date of birth for personal security reasons as it is part of your identity and I avoid business names or areas of expertise as these could change in the future.

If you have a well-known handle on other social media, you could consider this as an option as well "networkingsue" but I still recommend including your full name. Modifying your URL optimizes your name in search engine results and looks much better on your email signature, website, printed or digital business card, résumé or curriculum vitae etc.

Some people have multiple names and depending on which country they are looking for work in, they may like to only use two names rather than all of their personal and family names on their LinkedIn Profile and

URL. Some people may like to include a former name (before they were married) as they may be well known by this previous name.

You can change your URL at https://www.linkedin.com/public-profile/settings. **I believe this is one of the most important settings to change on LinkedIn for your future success** and essential for every LinkedIn User.

5.2 LinkedIn Profile Visibility

At https://www.linkedin.com/public-profile, you can turn your LinkedIn Profile visibility off or on. If you turn it off and someone has a link to your LinkedIn Profile, they will still see your LinkedIn Profile, but if they are looking for you in a search query, they will not see you. If you want to hibernate your LinkedIn Profile for a while and stop anyone from seeing you at all, you can go to https://www.linkedin.com/psettings/account-preferences and choose 'Hibernate' which will temporarily deactivate your Profile (there is no need to delete your Profile but you will need to remove yourself from any Groups or Pages that you manage to turn on Hibernate).

I do not recommend deleting your Profile for any reason (apart from when you pass away and your Digital Executor closes the Profile). I recommend changing your Headline details to say whatever it is you wish to achieve or not achieve on LinkedIn throughout your life. It could also be a handy reference tool for your eulogy and a way to let people know that you have passed away (please ensure that your Executor can gain access to your LinkedIn Profile by giving them access to a list of all of your online passwords. Mine are printed and placed securely with my will). I am hopeful that LinkedIn will create a 'legacy' version in the future as many people have had outstanding careers or businesses and whilst they may not have a Wikipedia page, hopefully they can have a LinkedIn Legacy Page showcasing their story and some of their most popular Posts and Articles.

5.3 Public Visibility

At https://www.linkedin.com/public-profile, you can decide if your LinkedIn Profile Photo is visible to the public (I recommend Yes) and whether or not you would like the other sections of your LinkedIn Profile to be publicly visible. Unless there is a particular security reason, I would normally suggest that you turn all of these On (you may need to check this every so often as sometimes they turn off without warning when the LinkedIn Platform is updated).

I have had some clients who have been a victim of domestic violence or criminal behavior or have a high security position and they need to live a very private life. For these clients, I recommend that they use a distant and low resolution LinkedIn Profile Photo, consider changing their name online, not providing the full details of their current employment in their LinkedIn Profile and adjusting the 'Who can see your Connections' to 'Only you.' However, I do believe that these clients should be able to retain access to their network and if they are concerned at any time, recommend that they either change their Public Visibility to No or Hibernate their LinkedIn Profile so that it cannot be seen by anyone until their situation changes.

5.4 Account Preferences

At https://www.linkedin.com/psettings/account-preferences there are a variety of options and I normally recommend turning Autoplay videos off at https://www.linkedin.com/psettings/videos to save the internet data allowance on your mobile device. Decide what works for you for the rest of the options.

5.5 Viewers Of This Profile Also Viewed

The default setting here is 'On' at https://www.linkedin.com/psettings/browse-map but I recommend 'Off.' If you leave this one turned on and I visit your LinkedIn Profile and start reading it, but then notice someone else's name and details that look interesting on my screen, I may go and look at their LinkedIn Profile instead of looking through all of your LinkedIn Profile. This is a good one to turn on late at night so that you can see who you may be competing with in the online world and then turning it back off again immediately after you have completed your own espionage.

5.6 Account Access

Email Address – I recommend adding all of your current and past email addresses to your LinkedIn Profile so that you do not accidentally create a Duplicate LinkedIn Profile https://www.linkedin.com/psettings/email. Do not worry that you cannot verify them if you no longer have access to them. I also like to encourage this process so that if someone you know syncs their phone or their email contacts with LinkedIn, the sync process can help 'find' you on LinkedIn and they can connect with you.

Please make sure that your Primary email address can receive email correspondence. You may prefer to choose your personal email address as the Primary email address if you are looking for work and your business email address if you are looking to secure business or are mostly using LinkedIn for business purposes.

Be aware that some high security roles do not allow you to add your work email address anywhere (especially government roles).

If you add your phone number at https://www.linkedin.com/psettings/phone, you can set up two factor authentication https://www.

linkedin.com/psettings/two-step-verification to reduce the likelihood of your LinkedIn Profile being hacked and also to help you gain access to your LinkedIn Profile if you lose access to your email address.

Be warned though that LinkedIn may ask you to sync your phone contacts with LinkedIn once they have your phone number and I do not recommend this process. You can unsync at https://www.linkedin.com/mynetwork/settings/manage-syncing.

5.7 Visibility

Profile viewing options – If you are using the free LinkedIn Profile, you will need to leave yourself 'turned on' at https://www.linkedin.com/psettings/profile-visibility if you would like to see the last five people who have looked at your LinkedIn Profile (and I recommend that you do this).

However, if you have a meeting tomorrow and you would like to look at someone's LinkedIn Profile and make sure that they do not know that you have looked at them, you can turn yourself to 'Anonymous' first. Even if they have a paid Premium Profile, they will not see that you have looked at them.

I sometimes do this when I am looking at a LinkedIn Profile for a client, but I actually like people to know that I have looked at them, because there is a 30% chance they will then look back at me so this can be a useful cold-calling technique. I do not see the value of the middle 'private profile characteristics' option – and I prefer to list myself as either On or Off.

If you have a Premium Profile, you can keep yourself Anonymous at all times and still look at other LinkedIn Profiles and see who has viewed your LinkedIn Profile. But remember, you may be missing out on people looking back at you because if you are Anonymous, they won't know that you have visited their LinkedIn Profile.

If you are on the free LinkedIn Profile, remember to turn it back On after you have finished looking around so that you can see the last five people who have viewed your LinkedIn Profile.

5.8 Who Can See Or Download Your Email Address

I am on LinkedIn to attract opportunities so I make my email address viewable in this section to Anyone on LinkedIn https://www.linkedin.com/psettings/privacy/email. However, if I was the CEO of a major organization, I would not!

I do not allow my email address to be downloaded during a LinkedIn data export because I want to avoid my email address being added to email lists that I did not subscribe to.

5.9 Who Can See Your Connections

Once again, because I am on LinkedIn to attract opportunities, I am comfortable allowing connections to see who I am connected to https://www.linkedin.com/psettings/connections-visibility.

However, if I was very high profile individual, in sales or concerned about privacy for personal reasons, I would choose 'Only you.' If it was set to 'Only you' and I was connected to Jane and she was connected to Simon, I would not see that Simon was part of Jane's network unless I was also connected to Simon. This means that the 'Only you' setting will only show your Shared Connections with that person.

5.10 Manage Active Status

Would you like people to know when you are online? If so, you can make that visible at https://www.linkedin.com/psettings/presence.

5.11 Share Job And Education Changes And Work Anniversaries

If you are about to update your LinkedIn Profile after not doing this for quite some time, I would suggest you turn this one off https://www.linkedin.com/psettings/activity-broadcast. You don't want to share a job update from three years ago with your Connections now. You can also turn this on individually when you update a section of your LinkedIn Profile.

5.12 Communications

There are a huge range of choices here for you to consider https://www.linkedin.com/psettings/communications. It is important for you to select your preferences because otherwise, you may end up with a lot of unwanted emails or notifications from LinkedIn that disrupt your daily activities.

Some people set up an email rule on their Inbox so that all messages from LinkedIn.com go to one folder and they check all of them at once. Others set a time limit every time they login to a social media platform or only check in once a day. If you choose to pay for a Premium LinkedIn Profile, more people can contact you if you have selected an Open Profile at https://www.linkedin.com/psettings/message-preferences.

One of the Communications settings I have changed is about receiving an individual email each time someone would like to connect with me. I receive several requests per day and as you can imagine, I do not want to receive an individual email for each request (only a Notification). I log on to LinkedIn most days (but I don't expect you to) and I take care of these Connection requests when I click on the My Network icon on the top menu.

5.13 Data Privacy

There are also a lot of different choices for you to consider here in relation to how your data is used by LinkedIn and third party sources and I won't go through them all https://www.linkedin.com/psettings/data-privacy. However, I do encourage you to be fully present and aware when you make your personal choices and when you select your Job Seeking Preferences.

5.14 Advertising Data

This section has a lot of settings turned on that you may not realize and if you do look at them, you may realize that you would prefer to turn them off. Please take a few moments to make your own choices, particularly in relation to Third Party Data https://www.linkedin.com/psettings/advertising-data.

As I said earlier, I have not gone through all of the settings you can adjust on your LinkedIn Profile as so many of these are a personal preference and only you can decide what is right for you.

If you have a very private personality, you may prefer settings that don't show when you are online. If you are after sales, you may prefer to have as many notifications as possible. It is up to you and your values, strengths and context as well as your values, purpose, goals and objectives for LinkedIn.

Also remember that these settings are likely to change in the future so you need to set a calendar reminder to check them once every six months as the settings are often changed automatically when there is an update to the LinkedIn platform and the updated default setting may be different to the preference you chose previously (and be changed without you doing anything or being notified of the change).

You may also like to review the settings for your other social media platforms now too.

6. Searches, Keywords, Algorithms And Hacks

In many respects, your LinkedIn Profile is like your own mini website and your Headline, which appears under your name, is the most important field for describing your value and values.

To help you collect the information you will ultimately need on your LinkedIn Profile, I invite you to use Appendix A at the back of the book.

To complete your LinkedIn Profile, you need to choose the various words you want to be found for online including the following:

- Your location.
- Your name.
- Your value offering, specialty, industry or profession.
- Your business or enterprize name (your own or where you work).

6.1 Searches

6.1.1 Location

I have started with location as all search engines have location as the very first criteria in search results. If I am in Melbourne, Victoria, Australia and I am looking for an accountant, it is not going to show me someone in my search results that is based in Sydney, New South Wales, Australia unless there are no accountants in Melbourne with a LinkedIn Profile and Sydney is the next nearest location (which it isn't). I have also chosen 'Greater Melbourne' rather than just 'Melbourne' as that would limit my appearances in search results to those in the Central Business District.

I understand that many of us are global citizens when it comes to work and can service clients from multiple countries. In this case, you may choose a country name rather than a state or territory name as your location. Remember though that search engines will also be using location as their first criteria as well. If your LinkedIn location matches your other online content, this will help you. Whilst I have chosen Greater Melbourne on LinkedIn and my actual suburb on my website, I have chosen Australia on my Google Business Account.

The good news is that I attract international work based on my keyword optimization, not my physical location. So consider your keywords and becoming really well known for them if you would like international gigs. This means that you will need to have content published on multiple websites and social media platforms from around the world to rank in search engine results in multiple locations.

At the end of the day, I have to say that I most enjoy working hyper locally, with people who live or work within a 10 kilometer radius of where I live. This helps me feel like a valuable member of my local community and helps people remember what I do and how I can help them which leads to more referrals. Whilst there are many advocates for 'working-from-home' I enjoy 'working-close-to-home.'

6.1.2 Name

Your name is relatively easy to be found in search engine results if you have updated your LinkedIn Profile URL (Section 5.1) if your name has a unique spelling. If you have a name that is in regular use by many people or there is someone else online who is well recognized for the same name, it is a good idea to try and personalize your name in some way. You could possibly include your middle name initial in all of your online social media profiles and handles e.g. 'Sam J Smith' or '@samjsmith' rather than 'Sam Smith.' You can also include pre nominals 'Dr Sam J Smith' or post nominals 'Sam J Smith MD.'

6.1.3 Value Offering

Deciding what you want to be found for is all about really understanding your values, strengths and context and your main values, purpose, goals and objectives for being on LinkedIn (Section 3).

By way of example, I provide a range of expertise in several different areas, but I have decided to give myself the 'label' of 'Independent LinkedIn Specialist.' When I was 'Sue Everything' I didn't attract opportunities because nobody could remember 'everything' that I did.

The word Independent is used because I do not work for LinkedIn and I want to make this very clear. LinkedIn is the area where I can provide the most value for my clients (career or business) and the word is easily remembered and recognized.

Specialist is my level of competency (this word cannot be used in every industry as some professions require formal accreditation before the word 'specialist' can be used).

As a result of being very specific in this label, it is quite clear about the value I offer when I appear in the LinkedIn Newsfeed, in content online and during any social media engagements (Reactions, Comments, Reposts). Over time, I have become memorable and recognizable with my 'label.' I also use the LinkedIn word a lot in both my LinkedIn Profile and LinkedIn Page and the Posts and Articles I write.

At the time of publishing this book, a search engine search for 'LinkedIn Specialist' anywhere in Australia shows a link to my online content in three positions on the first page of search engine results, with my LinkedIn

Profile being number one and my https://sueellson.com website in another two results. I will only keep this position in search engine results if I continue to add content and engage around the topic of LinkedIn in the future and people continue to click and find value when they click on the links (calculated by how long they spend on the page they look at).

The exciting news is that even though I have chosen 'Independent LinkedIn Specialist,' as my 'label,' I still attract a variety of other work in related disciplines – I haven't niched myself too much. However, by having a memorable label, I attract referrals and people can recall my name long after they have met me because I always appear with the label 'Independent LinkedIn Specialist' in the Newsfeed.

You can change your 'label' whenever you like and you may choose a different format for different reasons. I may change mine too. However, I would encourage you to incorporate your keywords, not just a value statement or some quirky copy that only makes sense if someone reads it. You need to be found first. Learn more about the main label to use in your Headline in Section 7.4.

6.1.4 Business Or Enterprize Name

If you have read my LinkedIn Profile, you will see that I have established two social enterprizes https://NewcomersNetwork.com in 2001 and https://CamberwellNetwork.com from 2012 to 2022. I am on the first page of search engine results for these names and this has been helped by having LinkedIn Pages.

6.1.5 LinkedIn Or Search Engine Searches

If you enter words in the Search field box on the top of your LinkedIn screen and press Enter, it will bring up a new screen and you can look for those words in the categories of People, Companies, Posts, Groups, Products, Jobs, Services, Events, Courses, Schools and All Filters.

Like every online search engine, LinkedIn wants to give you the most relevant and reliable search results. So it is probably no surprise that if you are looking for a Person, you are most likely to see somebody who is a First Level Connection (connected to you) who has those same words in their LinkedIn Profile Headline or their Current Job Title on the first page of your LinkedIn Search Results.

This is why I believe it is a good idea to connect with everyone you meet on LinkedIn *from now on* as it would be nice to work with someone you have already met (and it is impossible to remember everyone you have met and what they do).

The next level of search will show you Second level Connections – people connected to people you are already connected to and then Third level Connections which are people connected to one of your Second Level Connections. If you are using the free version of LinkedIn, you may not see the names of Third Level Connections in your LinkedIn Search Results.

I cannot provide you with the full rationale of the LinkedIn Search Results as I do not have that inside knowledge. To make these suggestions, I am relying on my experience of the LinkedIn platform. If you are not connected with someone with that skill set, I have noticed that the most likely result will show someone with those skills that is close to you location-wise.

Finally, regardless of what the LinkedIn Search Results show, it is still up to you to look at the person's LinkedIn Profile and do your own due diligence before engaging with them.

There are plenty of other searches you can do via the Search facility and if you have purchased either a LinkedIn Premium subscription or Sales Navigator, you can conduct more complex and comprehensive searches within LinkedIn. I find looking for Events and Content can be really interesting, especially when such a small percentage of users currently add Content or Events to the platform.

If you are having difficulty finding information via the LinkedIn Search field, you can complete a Google Advanced Search via https://www.google.com.au/advanced_search and put the words you are looking for in the top search field and the website LinkedIn.com in the Site field. You now have unlimited searches and this can be very helpful for research or sales prospecting.

All LinkedIn and search engine results are limited by what people include in the content they have on LinkedIn. This is why keywords are so important and if people **don't tell, they can't sell.** Quirky narratives can be fascinating to read but totally worthless if they don't allow you to be found for your keywords in the first place.

6.2 Keywords

A keyword can either be one word or a group of two to five words (sometimes called a keyword string). I know that seems confusing. If you have several keywords, it could be several lots of one word and/or several lots of two to five words. For my LinkedIn is a keyword but so is Career Specialist (two words).

If you are looking for work, you need to consider what your keywords will be. If you are at the beginning of your career, you can say that you are an 'Aspiring Accountant' or 'Future Accountant' whilst you are studying or looking for your first position and you will still appear in search results for 'Accountant.' I discuss this later in Section 7.4.

In this case, 'Accountant' is a primary keyword. However, there are also secondary keywords that can help you be found. These keywords need to focus on the additional value you provide. They could include words like Tax, Reporting, Budgeting, Strategy, Audit (related to tasks you would complete as an accountant) as well as technical competency related to accounting software (here in Australia that could be Xero, Quickbooks, MYOB).

You might be wondering how to work out your primary and secondary keywords. You need to start with what you believe decision-makers will be using to find someone with your skills. It is more likely to include common words rather than unique words. Coming up with some fancy title like 'Numbers Geek with a Green Pen' may sound really cool on some promotional material but it will not help you in a search query for an 'Audit Accountant!'

6.2.1 Finding Primary and Secondary Keywords

Primary keywords are the individual words or groups of two to five words that you **most** want to be found for and indicate where you can add the most value and are words that your searchers would most likely use in a typed or spoken search query.

Primary and Secondary Keywords can be found in a variety of places:

- Selected job advertisements.
- Selected job descriptions and key selection criteria.
- Job information or career specialist websites that provide descriptions for different occupations.
- Other people's LinkedIn Profiles including peers, mentors and consultants in your profession or industry (you may wish to go Anonymous (Section 5.7) to do this or let people know you are looking in case it leads to them looking at your LinkedIn Profile).
- Websites in your industry or profession (right click your mouse on a blank part of a website page, choose 'View Page Source' and look at the page title, keywords and meta description. If you are in business, this technique is usually part of a competitor or collaborator analysis).
- Magazines, publications and journals for the industry or profession.
- Job aggregator websites that curate content from multiple locations for jobs, tasks, industries or professions. These websites are also called gig platforms, career search engines, job crawlers and job spiders.

- Online tools that are used by website developers and search engine optimization specialists as well as resources built to help with content production and keyword generation (like Google AdWords).

- Talking to recruiters, people in the industry, attending live or online events, conferences and podcasts – wherever you can hear the current jargon for your profession or industry.

6.2.2 Selecting Your Secondary Keywords

Secondary keywords are designed to complement your Primary Keywords. They fall into various categories and have different purposes.

Search algorithms (mathematical equations designed to produce the best results) work on multiple factors. Ensuring that you have these Secondary Keywords in your LinkedIn Profile will give you the best chance for coming up in search results that are aligned with your Primary Keywords.

As I describe these Secondary Keywords, I will give you examples related to someone who is a Senior Human Resources Generalist (primary keyword) with a range of specialties (secondary keywords).

Related Keywords are words that are associated with your primary keywords. They are likely to be words that define your specialty area or niche and could be used to find you directly based on this area of expertise (e.g. Organizational Development, Change Management).

Technical Keywords if your career or business requires you to be able to use certain software or equipment, to achieve a particular Certification or License or to be a Member of a governing body, then including this information in your LinkedIn Profile is essential (HR Association Member, HRIS, Oracle).

New Keywords are words that replace the old keywords that may have been used in the past. Every industry and profession is regularly updating their common use terms, so if you want to be viewed as 'current,' you need to be using them too (e.g. People and Culture, Talent Management).

Old Keywords are words that may still be in use but they are not used as frequently as either the current keywords or new keywords. If you continue to use these and someone wants to search via that term, you may be the only person who appears in search results! (e.g. Personnel, Staffing, Workforce Management).

Descriptive Keywords are directly aligned to give more definition to your primary keywords. They are also qualifying words to help people understand more about your skills and they can help differentiate you from other people (e.g. Senior, Certified Professional, Manager, Experienced).

Positioning Keywords are keywords that help them say 'absolutely yes' or 'absolutely no.' If you have a certain style or preference, be open and frank about this up front so that the right people do contact you and the wrong people don't. Why waste time going through an unnecessary qualification process? You could have simply stated your preferences up front and saved your time and the other person's time. These words are often adjectives that describe you in more detail (e.g. Proactive, Business Focused, Inclusive, Consultative, Perceptive).

Culturally Appropriate Keywords these keywords may need to be added or removed depending on your location. Try not to make any particular assumptions about a location without qualified advice. Some industries and locations are very particular about the language they use in that particular location (e.g. Willing to travel, Current Availability, Language Skills, Can Work From Home WFH, Available Remotely).

Standard Keywords are keywords that you would always include regardless of your location, profession or industry. Just as Google wants every website to have an About Us and a Contact Us page, I would suggest that certain content must always be added to your LinkedIn Profile (e.g. your email address or preferred methods of contact, your call to action (CTA), what you want the right people to do once they have read your LinkedIn Profile and so on).

You need to:

- Consider the target audience you are trying to attract.
- Know the search terms they will use to search for you.
- Understand what content they want to view and include it.
- Invite them to take the next step in alignment with your goals.

6.2.3 Repeating Your Keywords

You also need to repeat your primary and secondary keywords, in context and in line with your purpose several times (but not just to fool the algorithm, it still needs to be in context).

Naturally, a LinkedIn Profile with particular keywords featured frequently is more likely to come up in search results than a LinkedIn Profile that only has the keywords mentioned a few times.

If your LinkedIn Profile is not coming up on the first page of search engine results for your keywords when you do a search, then you know that your keywords may not be in the best locations or repeated as often as necessary or you may not be very active online across multiple platforms or websites.

When you perform a search for a person (or an Advanced LinkedIn search for a person), the keywords you have chosen will appear on the screen on the search results page and this gives you some extra clues as to where on your LinkedIn Profile you can feature your keywords.

6.2.4 Location Of Your Keywords

The LinkedIn Algorithm is regularly changing and deciding where the most important locations are for your keywords.

From my experience, the highest priority locations include the Headline (directly underneath your name), your Current Position Job Title and your Past Position Job Title. Various other sections have indeterminate ranking after that, but can include your About section, your Experience description fields, your Education description fields, your Voluntary Experience description fields, your Skills (a field often used by recruiters) and possibly even the words in your Recommendations and the words in the LinkedIn Profiles of your Connections, particularly those that have similar words or Endorsements for the same Skills.

It may feel counter-intuitive to connect with your competitors on LinkedIn. However, LinkedIn is a very large database and databases like similar information to provide more accurate results. So the irony is that the more competitors, peers and colleagues that you are connected to, the more likely the algorithm is to believe that your specialty value is authentic!

If these competitors, peers or colleagues with similar Skills endorse you for the same Skills they have, well done. If you know that these people have similar Skills to you and you have seen them use those skills, then consider endorsing them as well. Practice the abundance philosophy rather than the scarcity philosophy. Although I love being a LinkedIn Specialist, I can't look after everyone so I happily endorse other LinkedIn Specialists for their Skills (provided I have seen their skills in action)!

The only time I recommend that you reduce the number of keywords you have on your LinkedIn Profile is if you have a significant public presence and you find yourself being inundated with unwanted correspondence and your main call to action does not redirect viewers effectively. In this instance, you may want to turn off your LinkedIn Profile Visibility (Section 5.2) but you do not want to delete your LinkedIn Profile and lose your Connections.

6.3 Algorithms

Algorithms give higher ranking to fully completed and regularly accessed and engaging LinkedIn Profiles. So if you have only decided to use LinkedIn for the next month whilst you are desperately seeking a new opportunity and then forget all about it, you are less likely to attract opportunities on a regular basis.

I am not trying to railroad you into logging on to LinkedIn every day, but if you do login at least once a week, it is much more likely to keep your network alive and keep your LinkedIn Profile attractive to the algorithm, particularly if you engage with the Newsfeed (React, Comment and Repost and Post) and keep up to date with your Connection invitations, Messages and Notifications.

Apart from the ways LinkedIn collects information to provide the best user experience, it also monitors your activity (signals) to help LinkedIn determine who and what is of most interest to you and what will appear in your Newsfeed.

If I start engaging with Posts from writers, then I will start to see more Posts from writers. If I spend a lot of dwell time over certain content, then my behavior is letting LinkedIn know what interests me and I will probably see more of it. If I connect to a new person and don't engage with their Newsfeed content in the first two weeks of our online 'relationship,' I may never see their content again. If I really want to see their content in the future, then I should click on the Notification Bell on their LinkedIn Profile.

Our online behavior is tracked to ensure we have a positive experience on the platform. The LinkedIn algorithms are also designed to weed out the people who are not playing by the rules. No-one is immune, so please, abide by the LinkedIn User Agreement.

6.4 Hacks

Over the years, a range of hacks (techniques designed to gather even more value from LinkedIn) have appeared and then once the developers have identified them, they disappear to ensure that the platform remains user friendly and provides a safe experience. If users have a negative experience on LinkedIn, then they are less likely to use it in the future, or they may even leave it. Bad behavior hurts the platform for everyone, even the abusers.

I have discovered a few helpful hacks quite by accident from time to time. For example, I discovered that if I updated my LinkedIn Headline on my iPhone, I had more characters available than if I updated it on my laptop or desktop computer.

That hack no longer works because the number of characters available in the Headline is the same for the iPhone or tablet via the LinkedIn App or the laptop or desktop version of LinkedIn.

I have discovered some features that are only available on the LinkedIn App on a mobile device that are not available via the laptop or desktop computer internet browser version and this may always be the case as the technology used for the LinkedIn App is different to the technology used for an internet browser and it may be different again in the future as new forms of the internet evolve.

If you provide professional services related to helping other people use LinkedIn, I encourage you to be observant at all times and test out how well certain techniques work for you. If you have started reading content provided by other LinkedIn trainers and specialists, you will quickly realize that we all have our own methodologies for maximizing the use of LinkedIn.

Wherever possible, I explain my reasons and rationale for my recommendations and I encourage my students and clients to quiz me if they have a different view on how to use LinkedIn (either their own view or a view from someone else).

If you find information that is contradictory to what I have suggested in this book, as I mentioned in the Disclaimer at the beginning of the book, I encourage you to ask the person providing that suggestion why they believe it is important and then decide for yourself which technique you would like to use for your own values, purpose, goals and objectives, provided it is within the rules of the LinkedIn User Agreement.

Overall, as mentioned previously, I adopt the principle of being 'friendly and professional' at all times on LinkedIn. I like to see myself as someone who provides helpful and educational content in a user-friendly way because I am an Author, Educator, Practitioner and Consultant.

I do not believe LinkedIn should be used for personal content. This type of content is better suited to other social media platforms. That is not to say you cannot incorporate personal stories and emotion in your content, but I would definitely steer clear of posting pictures of food, animals, children or holiday destinations on LinkedIn.

By way of example, several years ago, I was looking for an image to talk about LinkedIn. At the time, I was looking after a foster cat called George and he jumped up on my desk and sat next to my laptop where I was using LinkedIn. I quickly took a photo and posted it on LinkedIn saying that 'George wants to be on LinkedIn.'

It was meant to be something light-hearted and fun, but I was quickly admonished by a LinkedIn User who suggested that pictures of cats were not appropriate on LinkedIn. Another LinkedIn User came to my defense, but I learnt my lesson very quickly.

Some people ask themselves before they post any content online, 'Would my mother approve of this type of content?' before hitting the publish button. I prefer to ask myself, 'is this content adding authentic and aligned value?' If yes, then I happily share it. If no, I usually delete it because I find that it is usually a 'vanity' click-bait piece or a 'humble brag' that doesn't provide the reader with any specific value. You can ask for a 'sale' on LinkedIn, but you don't need to push for one at every opportunity either.

There are LinkedIn Specialists around the world who do all sorts of testing to determine how to use the LinkedIn algorithm to their advantage – to either be found in search results or to have their content go more viral.

Whilst I agree in principle with this testing and analysis, I would still like to believe that as a LinkedIn User, the most useful information related to my activities will appear during my online experience thanks to the LinkedIn algorithm that is constantly being tweaked and is based on a lot of LinkedIn User signal and behavior data, way beyond any amount of testing I could do. If I stay up to date and keep attracting the opportunities I seek, I would say that LinkedIn is working for me.

Ultimately, my number one hack for LinkedIn is to simply be consistent. Chasing shiny objects or perfect techniques can be a real time waster. For example, if one Post goes particularly well, be happy. If an Article receives a lot of Comments, make sure you reply to all of them. But show up again next week regardless. You can't rely on any one activity to provide you with unlimited resources forever.

I have had some Posts receive up to 35,000 impressions. Others, lucky to receive 350. I don't lie awake at night worrying about it because I know for a fact, sometimes they work and sometimes they don't. I just carry on with my consistent approach.

If you are contacted by someone via LinkedIn, please remain polite and respectful at all times, even if their approach has been inappropriate. If they have breached the LinkedIn User Agreement, I Report and Block them immediately lest they destroy the LinkedIn goose laying those golden eggs.

If you discover techniques that perform better, celebrate and consider re-using them provided no-one is affected negatively. Be willing to analyze and review your efforts every so often.

By way of example, there was a belief that if you included a link to another website in your Post in the Newsfeed, the Post would not go as viral. So people started posting content and told people to look in the Comments for the link. The LinkedIn User experience level dropped to zero at this point. Whilst your Post views may increase, the referrals to your website are likely to decrease. If I am interested in your content, I want to be able to click on the link immediately, not hunt and peck around the Comments.

They then decided on an alternative idea and edited their Post shortly after publication and added the link in to the body of the Post. It might have 'fooled' the algorithms for a while, but to be honest, if I ever see an edited Post, I am always suspicious as to why it needed to be edited, so I would probably never click on the link anyway. (If I make a typing mistake that I recognize immediately after posting, I delete the Post and start again).

I like to ensure that if someone reads my content online, they can learn something without having to click somewhere else to gain some value. If they do click, they may find more information, but preferably, they get something instantly from just reading the Post or Article. This ensures that I remain authentic and professional at all times.

Learning some fancy hacks may work for a certain period of time, but they eventually get 'found out' and you can spend your whole life chasing a silver bullet that doesn't exist (or disappears soon after you find it) or you can get on with just turning up and being authentic on a regular basis and you will develop a credible reputation that is far better than a quick win here and there.

A few years ago, video was extremely popular and some people started posting a lot of videos. Naturally, they didn't have enough content to do it frequently and then they started over-sharing about their personal lives. It was awful. Most of them disappeared soon after. Thankfully there is now a much better mix of video and non-video content in the Newsfeed.

If you want the latest and greatest tips and tricks, I recommend that you look for a LinkedIn Specialist, view their LinkedIn Profile and Recent Activity and decide if they can give you a professional update and save you the time and effort of working it out for yourself (just as you hire an Accountant for your financial matters, a LinkedIn Specialist can help you with maximizing LinkedIn).

If you really want to maximize LinkedIn, I would suggest that you book an appointment with a LinkedIn Specialist every three or six months to ensure you are up to date with the latest insights and offerings.

Hopefully, with this understanding of 'how' LinkedIn works, you can get on with the doing. Up until now, I have discussed the points that relate to you whether you are looking for assistance with your work, career, business or enterprize.

In the next chapter, I will look at more specific components of your LinkedIn Profile and options for each section.

7. Your Personal LinkedIn Profile

Do you like filling in forms? If yes, fantastic! If not, you may like to have a look at Appendix 1 in the back of this book so that you can collect the information you need before you start filling in or updating your LinkedIn Profile.

It can take quite a lot of time to complete all of these sections and you might like to start with the 'easiest' first (the Languages section!).

I have provided a range of reasons for my suggestions and you are most welcome to choose other options (provided you abide by the LinkedIn User Agreement). I always believe that 'some information' is better than no information, so if you start with some basic details, you can fill in the rest over time.

I have spent many hours over the years tweaking my content as my goals have changed. Unlike writing a book that remains static, your LinkedIn Profile can be as dynamic as you are! I describe online content as a 'Version Number.' Today, it is Version 1.0, next week, Version 1.1. Later on with a significant change, it could be Version 2.0 then Version 2.1 etc.

Your other goal is to complete as many sections as possible so that the right query can help you be found for the right opportunity. This will also give you the opportunity to showcase your digital competency and attract better search results in LinkedIn and via the internet as there will be more information that describes your value in more sections.

Depending on the length of your career, it could take many hours to complete your LinkedIn Profile according to the suggestions in this book. If you see this task as an opportunity to provide a guided reflection on what you have achieved, you will gain new insights as you remember the people you worked with, the tasks you have completed and the different enterprizes where you have worked.

It can be a great tool for deciding what you would like to do next (as you reflect on your past experiences). Once you have completed your LinkedIn Profile, all you need to do is tweak it every now and then and update it when new information is available. Make sure you save your LinkedIn Profile to PDF along the way so that you can go back and visit previous versions at any time. Remember to make sure that anything that does not appear in the PDF has been saved as well (you may like to have a Document or Spreadsheet with all of your data).

So let's get started...

7.1 Your Name

It might seem like a simple field to fill in, your 'name' on your LinkedIn Profile. However, some people have chosen to include additional keywords or business names in the name field and this is against the LinkedIn User Agreement and puts them at risk of having their LinkedIn Profile suspended or deleted without warning. I also believe it interferes with name search results.

Whilst you could include post nominals in your name field (like MBA), I believe it is more appropriate to include these in your Headline, About and Education sections.

A former name (like a maiden name for a person who is now married and using their partner's surname) can be included and it will appear in brackets and allow a person to be found for their current name or former name. This is very helpful for people completing family tree research or for people who have a significant body of work or personal network under a previous name.

Next to your name, you can also include your gender pronouns. I have chosen to include she/her in solidarity with people who want to be recognized by particular pronouns. Some people choose to use this field for alternative purposes but I do not recommend it as it is against the intention of the field.

In the LinkedIn App on your mobile device (phone or tablet), you can also add an audio pronunciation of your name. You may also choose to mention something else within the 10 seconds (like your title or 'label' from your LinkedIn Headline). When you do this, a speaker icon will appear next to your name.

7.2 Profile Photo

LinkedIn Profile Viewers will spend up to 60% of their time when they visit your LinkedIn Profile looking at your personal photo. To say it is important is probably an understatement!

What you wear, how you style your hair and where you have your photo taken really needs to match the type of opportunity you wish to attract on LinkedIn both now and in the future.

I understand that in some countries and in some professions a non-smiling passport style photo may be considered appropriate, but more generally, I would say that a smiling photo in color is the preferred option. I believe a smile is a universal sign that every person from every background understands.

I encourage my students and clients to wear a high neck garment for their photograph so that their face can be 'framed' by their clothing. This helps redirect the viewer to the most important part of your face, your eyes and not lower down to your neck or chest.

If you can have the top of your head at the top of the circle and your eyes sitting on the top one third line in the photo circle, this will also increase the quality of your presence in the circle and make it easier to see your face when your photograph appears as a small icon size picture in the Newsfeed or in a Search Result.

I also encourage you to use a color photograph rather than a black and white photograph as in some countries, black and white photos are only used on gravestones. Ideally you will not have a complex background, or jewelry or clothing that takes attention away from your eyes.

Contextual images (like wearing a hard hat, safety goggles and a high visibility vest for an Occupational Health and Safety Manager) or a workplace background behind you can really add a visual story to your LinkedIn Profile.

As more people consider multiple types of work, personal styling in a photograph can vary accordingly. A hands-on leader may feel constricted in a formal shirt and matching suit and may prefer a more casual top, jacket and pants. A hard rock musician may have a completely different visual appearance altogether.

Regardless of any of these suggestions, make sure you feel comfortable with the photo and make sure that it is appealing to the decision-makers you wish to convince. A professional photographer took over 70 photos before I found one I was happy to use at the time, so don't be surprised if you need to go above and beyond three quick shots on your phone to find a photo you feel comfortable using. I do not recommend including other people in the photograph.

When you add your photo, make sure you also ensure that your LinkedIn Profile Photo visibility is set to Public. If you would like to check your visibility, you can go to https://www.linkedin.com/public-profile/settings.

Additionally,, I am not a fan of the green Frame on your LinkedIn Profile Photo that says 'Open to Work' (which can be turned on or off at https://www.linkedin.com/in/YOURURL/opportunities/job-opportunities/onboarding) because I think it makes you appear 'desperate.' That is another choice entirely up to you. I like to let my keywords and my content do the talking. I do however have my Open to Work setting turned on so that Recruiters can approach me even though the green Frame is not visible.

If you would like to have your LinkedIn Profile Photo assessed before you add it to LinkedIn, you can use the website https://photofeeler.com and viewers can rate your likability, competence and influence. Please understand that this is largely an American audience of 'raters' and you still need to feel comfortable with the photo you choose. I have found that the final 'result' from the raters can vary quite considerably depending on who actually rates your photograph and when you stop accepting more votes.

In the LinkedIn App on your mobile device (phone or tablet), you will also see a plus + symbol next to your photo where you can add a 30 second Video Cover Story or the green Frame saying 'Open to work' or a purple Frame saying 'Hiring.'

You can either record the video in the LinkedIn App or select a video recording from your mobile device and you can also add stickers. This enables visitors to your LinkedIn Profile to learn more about you and usually creates a slightly different visual mark around your Profile Photo circle so that visitors know a video is available to watch.

7.3 Background Banner Image

In my view, almost anything is better than the default Background 'Banner' Image because it shows a lack of digital competency.

The quickest and easiest option is to create a white or LinkedIn blue HEX #0a66c2 or RGBA(10,102,194,255) color image that is 1584 (wide) x 396 (high) pixels in size.

You could add a favorite photo trimmed to these dimensions, but it is important not to have a Background Banner Image that is so interesting that people look at your Background Image instead of your Profile Photo (people like to 'buy' from people).

Another option is to choose a plain color that is also in your LinkedIn Profile Photo, perhaps one of the colors from the garment you are wearing or a color in the background of your photo. This can enhance the appearance of your face quite significantly if the right color is chosen.

Some people with a specific goal choose to add a logo, branding, main value proposition etc in the Background Banner Image. This is all entirely up to you. However, please check how the image appears on a phone or tablet to ensure it can still be read when your LinkedIn Profile Photo moves to the middle of the screen. You don't want your face to cut out important information. Likewise, LinkedIn does not want you to include advertising information in your Background Banner Image and if you do, they may turn off the visibility of your Background Banner Image.

7.4 Headline and Headline Formula

If you asked several different LinkedIn Specialists for their 'headline formula,' they would probably all give you a different formula suggestion.

Your number one priority is your purpose! What are you trying to be found for on LinkedIn and what do you want to be remembered for? If people didn't read anything else on your LinkedIn Profile, would they have some idea about how you provide value to others if they only read your Headline?

Here is the formula I use and recommend.

7.4.1. Memorable Label

When I gave myself the label 'Independent LinkedIn Specialist' (yes, I know, you should only label jars, not people!), I suddenly became memorable and started getting more work (and search engine results too I might add). It didn't stop me getting the range of work I currently enjoyed, it just helped people remember how I provide value and what is most aligned to what I do.

If you met me in person and asked me 'what do you do?' and I said I am a 'Plumber' you would probably remember that. But if I started rattling off that I am an author, educator, practitioner, consultant, trainer and gigster in the areas of careers, business, marketing and social media, you may be unlikely to remember me at all!

Likewise, if you are scrolling through the Newsfeed of LinkedIn, you will not see my full Headline in the Newsfeed. That is why the first three to five words are the most important. They are the words that most people will see regularly if you are active on LinkedIn.

So to break it up some more, my 'label' is Independent LinkedIn Specialist.

I chose the word 'Independent' to clarify my uniqueness.

I chose the word 'LinkedIn' to define my area of expertise.

I chose the word 'Specialist' to define my level of capability.

If you are looking for a specific role and it is more senior than your current role, you could use a word like 'Aspiring' or 'Future' as your clarifying word. e.g. Aspiring Scientist, Future Logistics Manager. This means you will appear in search results for your keyword 'Scientist' or 'Logistics Manager' even though you are not currently in that type of role.

This is also helpful if you are changing careers, because you can focus on being found for your future goals, not your existing tasks.

If you have more than one set of Primary Keywords, focus on the ones that are most relevant for what you want to achieve from LinkedIn. For example, you may currently be a Senior Project Manager but want to transition to a Contemporary Visual Artist. If you don't need to use LinkedIn to get another Project Management role, you could put Contemporary Visual Artist first in your Headline.

7.4.2. Primary Value Related Keywords

I love keywords and your Primary keywords should definitely be included in your Headline as this is the number one search priority field. Again, enter them in the order of importance for you and your values, purpose, goals and objectives.

Some people like to include a specific value statement - how you can provide value to an employer or a client. These words are not usually part of a search query, so I like to leave that information for the first three lines of the About section. I would rather include more specific keywords in the Headline and appear in more search results.

I like to capitalize each word in the Headline, say each word only once and come up with as many 'combinations' as possible from the full list. I use commas where needed rather than pipes | because you need a space either side (for a total of three characters) and a comma and space only takes two characters. A pipe also takes the eye up and then it has to come down again to read the next word which slows down the reading process and the comprehension of the words being read.

I also avoid using a slash / because it actually joins two words together so you won't be 'found' for either word in a search query. In computer language, if I write 'Owner/Operator,' the words will be merged into one word 'OwnerOperator' and you will not be found for either 'Owner' or 'Operator.' If you still want to use a slash, please put a space either side of the slash so it appears as 'Owner / Operator'.

I also avoid too much narrative or extra adjectives that would not be part of a search query in the Headline. My ultimate goal is to appear in more search results so that I can be viewed by more people and then make sure that the user experience when someone views my LinkedIn Profile helps them to understand whether we are a values fit or not.

Other good items to include are acronyms specific to your expertise or industry. e.g. a Project Manager could include PMP. Professional Association Membership status may also be appropriate e.g. FCAHRI - Fellow Certified Member of the Australian Human Resources Institute.

7.4.3. Personal Interest Word And/Or Emoji

LinkedIn is a social media platform for professionals, but that doesn't mean you have to be ALL professional and not a little social. If you can include a word and an emoji that reflects a personal interest of yours, when people read your LinkedIn Profile, they get to know a little bit more about you as a person and it can be a great conversation starter as you build new professional relationships online.

It also makes you more memorable and adds a little bit of color and flavor to your Headline and potentially helps you to stand out. Let me assure you that if you are looking at a lot of LinkedIn Profiles, they all start to look the same after a while. You want to be attractive to the right audience.

If you can't right click your mouse and insert an emoji on your laptop or desktop computer, you can search for an emoji online and copy and paste the emoji in to your Headline.

Please choose an aligned emoji. I once had an accountant who mentioned that one of his interests was playing poker. I don't know about you but I would not feel comfortable hiring an accountant who likes to gamble with money!

I have chosen a 'dancing woman' emoji for my LinkedIn Profile. As a 'woman of a certain age,' I want people to know that I am active physically! I only include one emoji at the end of my Headline because emojis appear as gobbledegook for people using assistive technology.

What to avoid in the Headline

Here's my list of what NOT to include in your Headline.

- Any version of 'Open To Opportunities' because searchers are going to use keywords to find someone and you will not appear in any relevant search results. It also makes you look desperate.
- Years of experience - it is irrelevant - focus on your skills.
- Too many emojis. Makes you look like a try-hard and cannot be read by assistive technology.
- Job Title and Company Name only. It makes you look like you don't know how to maximize LinkedIn and are not digitally competent enough to adjust it from the automatic selection of your current job role to your own keyword optimized statement.
- Spelling mistakes and inconsistencies (like not using capital letters in a consistent way).

- Using all capital letters. This is considered to be 'shouting' in the online world.

- Leaving it blank. That looks really bad and reduces your chance of appearing in any search results.

- Creating two LinkedIn Profiles. Your headline can talk about multiple specialties and you can be known for more than one area of expertise. Just put the one that is most important for your values, purpose, goals and objectives first.

- Words that are only known in your industry but not used by searchers looking for what you do. You may need to include 'consumer,' popular use words or job title words as well as industry words in your Headline.

- Losing your Headline. You may have gone to a lot of trouble to create a great Headline and if you have, I suggest you save a copy of it (perhaps email it to yourself) because if you change your work and add more Experience to your LinkedIn Profile, you may accidentally replace your Headline with your new Job Title. Oops. All that hard work, gone.

7.5 Contact Info

Your Contact Info link is in your top display area at https://www.linkedin.com/in/YOURURL/detail/contact-info and it needs to be completed. I have chosen to have my email address accessible to anyone on LinkedIn, so that it can appear in this section.

You can include three website links. Please open the website and copy/paste the link in from your internet browser, do not hand type it as you may not have the exact link. This is an ideal location for a link to an online form if you do not want to publish your email address.

If you do not have your own website, you can link to a website that is related to you in some way. It could be your current employer, a professional association where you are a member (or would like to be or have a profile page), a profile you have on another social media platform or even a free Google website that you have created via https://business.google.com. Anything that helps showcase your interests online.

In the Address field, I don't recommend including your personal home address, but you may like to mention your local suburb or town, city, state and country if you are looking for work. Alternatively, you could also use your current workplace address. This location is in addition to the postal or zip code you may have entered elsewhere and helps LinkedIn identify where you are in the world.

If you are currently in one location but want to move to another and attract opportunities in the new location, you can update your LinkedIn Profile location with where you want to work (so you can be found in that location's search results) as well as this Contact Info address field. In the About section, you could explain where you are now and when you are planning to move to the new location so that you are not 'lying' on your LinkedIn Profile.

If you would like to appear in search results for other locations, you can choose up to five locations at https://www.linkedin.com/in/YOURURL/opportunities/job-opportunities/onboarding. Likewise, if you are willing to travel or work remotely, you could also include this information in the About section.

If you have completed the Providing Services section, you can select your current location and say that you can work remotely.

If you have added a Twitter connection https://www.linkedin.com/psettings/twitter-accounts it will appear on this screen. You can also list an Instant Messaging Platform (Skype, ICQ, Google Hangouts, QQ or WeChat) and your birthdate, but I do not recommend including your birthdate for privacy and security reasons (it is part of your identity and can be used for fraud attempts).

7.6 About

Now here is a hot topic! Nearly everyone you speak to will have a different opinion on how you can write your About (Summary) section.

At present, the first three lines are visible without clicking 'see more.' For this reason, I suggest that you make it VERY clear what you want people to do if they are visiting your LinkedIn Profile in these first three lines. It is an ideal spot to put your main call-to-action CTA.

I include my contact details and a text based hyperlink to the Services page on my personal website. Whilst this link is not 'clickable' on a desktop or laptop computer, it is clickable when someone is viewing my LinkedIn Profile on an Android device and it can be copied and pasted if someone is genuinely interested in learning more.

If you are looking for work, you can start with your contact details and 'Interested in roles in...'

If you are looking for work but don't want everyone to know about it, you can start with your contact details and then say 'Specialties include...' By having your contact details immediately accessible, it shows recruiters and decision-makers that you are willing to be contacted. You may prefer to only mention your email address and not include your phone number.

If you are looking for business, you can start with how to purchase your goods or services.

If you are a senior leader who receives interest from the media, customers, shareholders or stakeholders, you could provide a link to a contact form that people can complete rather than share your personal details publicly.

If you choose to include a personal narrative, you can choose to write in the first person, third person or no person.

First person uses 'I,' e.g. 'I am a Social Media Marketing professional specializing in producing paid advertisements for various business clients.' A lot of people like this format because it appears more personal and friendly and after all, it is your LinkedIn Profile so people like to hear 'you' speaking.

However, you need to be careful not to use 'I' at the beginning of every sentence as this can be very repetitive and potentially sound as if it is 'all about you' and not about how you can provide value. Also, if I am reading about 'I', there is a chance I could be thinking about myself, but 'I' am reading about you...do you see where I am going with this?

If you choose the third person, the same sentence would be, 'Sam J Smith is a Social Media Marketing professional specializing in producing paid advertisements for various business clients.' This helps the person reading the text to understand what Sam does and helps them remember Sam's name and skills. This is my preferred option although some people feel it is impersonal. This text could also be used to introduce Sam if they were speaking at an event. Again, you wouldn't start every sentence with 'Sam,' you could use a preferred pronoun or just start with the next topic.

If you choose 'no' person, the same sentence would be, 'Social Media Marketing professional specializing in producing paid advertisements for various business clients.' Again, it can feel a bit impersonal, but it can feel more succinct and direct which may suit some people's preferences. It can also be useful for people who don't like using 'I' or their name and are a little more reluctant to reveal information online.

I strongly encourage you NOT to mention your years of experience. If you mention, '22 years of experience in international and domestic supply chain management, logistics and freight' and someone who is only 22 years old is reading your LinkedIn Profile, they will potentially believe you have too much experience (and you will need to update the number of years every year). If you mention 'five years of experience,' that could be too few for a senior role. The dates of your employment provide your years of experience and in a personal interview, you can provide specific details.

The option I recommend is to describe the type of experience you have. 'Extensive experience in international and domestic supply chain management, logistics, freight, shipping and trade.' It is a much better use of language. Now, you can potentially be seen as a 'guru' rather than a dinosaur. If you are still in the early stages of your career, you could say, 'Varied experience in international and domestic supply chain management, logistics and freight' and still be found for all of those lovely keywords.

For the remaining About text, I recommend a variety of different strategies for different people and likewise, you really need to think about what you are trying to achieve with your LinkedIn Profile and how you can attract the right people and encourage them to engage appropriately. It would also be good if the people who cannot benefit from your offering can self-identify and move on to the next LinkedIn Profile that is more aligned. Why would you want to attract contact from someone who is not a good fit for your values, purpose, goals and objectives and then answer their message or phone call?

For a typical job seeker looking for a full time position, I like to break up the About section into bullet points so that it is 'scan friendly' and easy to read and interpret on a small screen (like a mobile device) or a larger number of screens where potentially multiple candidates are being viewed at the same time (with a recruiter or decision-maker).

I would list headings including Professional Skills (related to your experience), Technical Skills (highlighting specific technologies you can use), Personal Skills (related to your unique personality and approach to work and sometimes called 'soft skills'), Industry Experience (if this includes multiple industries or professions), International Experience (if you have worked in multiple countries) and Personal Interests (that give some insight into you as a person).

It would appear like this:

Professional Skills
> skill a
> skill b
> skill c, etc

Technical Skills
> program a
> program b
> program c, etc

Personal Skills
> skill a
> skill b
> skill c, etc

Industry Experience
> industry a
> industry b
> industry c, etc

International Experience
> country a
> country b
> country c, etc

Personal Interests
> interest a
> interest b
> interest c, etc

These lists would also go in priority order with your current or future focus items listed at the top of each list and primary and secondary keywords included. It is up to you how many adjectives you use in this section but please remember that shorter bullet points are much easier to read, process, find and remember. Ideally, I would encourage each item to be less than five words.

Sorting each of these items into categories makes it easy to see how your skills match an opportunity. It also makes it easier to 'find' a skill set if it is sorted logically. The extra white space around the list of skills makes it much easier to read on a screen. You may have also noticed that I start each bullet point with a lower case letter as this makes it easier to read and no full stop at the end because that tells the reader to pause and we would like them to keep reading.

I believe that a brief narrative story after the bullet points can help the reader infer your level of capability and value by attaching the skills to your story. It can describe your career in a chronological or reverse chronological order or just focus on your most important message.

I have often suggested different time sequences.

For example, present, past and future. Sue Ellson is an Independent LinkedIn Specialist. Sue started work as a career recruit at Westpac Banking Corporation and has been self-employed in a variety of industries since 1994. In the future, she plans to concentrate on her writing career.

Alternatively, future, past, present. Sue Ellson is working toward a full time writing career. She started work as a career recruit for Westpac Banking Corporation and has been self-employed in a variety of industries since 1994. Sue is currently an Independent LinkedIn Specialist.

Finally, past, present, future. Sue Ellson started work as a career recruit at Westpac Banking Corporation and has been self-employed in a variety of industries since 1994. She is currently an Independent LinkedIn Specialist and is preparing for a future writing career.

For a business owner, a similar skills list can be used or you can focus on how you provide value. For my own service based enterprize, I have included free options (for those who cannot afford to pay for my services), low cost training or self-help options (for those who would like some assistance) and personalized premium options (for those who would like it done-with-them as I do not offer a done-for-you service).

If you are a product based business owner, you can go into more detail about your offerings before providing a personal narrative of your experience (in a biography format that can also be used to introduce you as a speaker or presenter or as a biography on a website or annual report).

I believe that making the story relatable to your ideal clients is very important. Visual language that helps people picture you in your various roles makes you more memorable. For example, 'Started my career stacking shelves in the local XYZ supermarket' creates a vivid imaginable picture.

You can include website links that have been copied and pasted from your internet browser in any of the text boxes on your LinkedIn Profile and these will appear as clickable links on an Android Device (as will phone numbers written with a + and the international dialing code). For users not using an Android Device, they can copy and paste the link into their own internet browser.

Do you have any certifications or accreditations that can make the person feel more comfortable with their buying decision? I like to include my education and membership post nominals after the first appearance of my name in the About section (for example Sue Ellson BBus MPC CDAA ASA WV SPN) for people who like to know this information up front.

Do you have any recent or significant honors or awards that are meaningful to your ideal clients, suppliers, stakeholders etc?

I remember reading a LinkedIn Profile that explained that the person was a bad golfer and that they were happy to be contacted and chat about business or golf. This made me smile but also made me feel as if the person was approachable and friendly. I was so intrigued that I almost contacted him even though I didn't need his services and I don't like golf!

If you are in a very senior executive role or are very well known, you may not have time to deal with direct contact from multiple people including employees, shareholders, media etc. In this case, you could direct people to your personal assistant or your manager or as mentioned before, an online website enquiry form with a lot of questions to filter out non-genuine enquiries.

I like including my contact details at the top in a 'mobile device' friendly format so that people can just click on their screen and reach me. This is very important if you are looking for work. If you don't want to have your phone number visible, you can just include your email address or preferred messenger identity.

Whatever you do, please make sure you have a call to action (CTA). It is a good idea to suggest what the visitor needs to do next. Visit your website? Make an appointment? Call you directly? Invite you for a job interview? Don't be afraid to provide instructions so that they know what to do next. If you don't want it to be obvious to your current employer, just include your contact details (like your personal email address) and see what happens!

As with all content you add to LinkedIn, it is better if it is 'format free.' For this reason, I 'wash' text copied from any other programs by pasting it into either Notepad on a Microsoft device or Text Edit on an Apple device, converting it to plain text and then pasting it into LinkedIn. This ensures that all of the text can be read by the LinkedIn search algorithms and any text formatting code is removed.

Some people use a Unicode Text Converter so that the text appears in a different font style on LinkedIn rather than just plain text. I do not recommend this strategy as I cannot confirm that the text will be 'read' by the LinkedIn Algorithm so you may find that you are then penalized in search queries.

Yes, emojis can be included in the text boxes, but please be aware that too many emojis can confuse the message or distract from your true intention and cannot be read by assistive technology. Remember that humor is not always universal, so please be careful when including humorous content.

If you are Open to New Opportunities or Open to Work you can type in here #ONO or #opentowork but please do not put any text like this in your Headline or at the beginning of your About section as it makes you look 'desperate.'

Before you press Save, proofread all of your content to avoid spelling and grammar mistakes. I also like to suggest that you copy and paste your content into your own document before you press Save just in case the system fails (and it has on me a few times). You don't want to lose all of that text you have just written due to a system error. Remember to Save your Profile to PDF every time you make significant changes to your LinkedIn Profile.

7.7 Resources (Visible Only To You) - Creator Mode

This section gives you the ability to turn on Creator Mode. If you are going to be sharing content on a regular basis, I highly recommend that you turn this on.

Creator Mode will change your 'Connect' button on your LinkedIn Profile to a 'Follow' button and invite you to nominate five topics that you talk about on a regular basis that are listed as hashtags and ideally, you will use these hashtags in your Posts reasonably often.

I recommend that one of the hashtags you choose be your unique hashtag name so that viewers of your Posts can click on the hashtag and see what else you have published. I have chosen #sueellson but other people have chosen a personalized hashtag that includes their name and their regular topic because their name may be used by someone else. For example #sueellsonlinkedinways.

Creator Mode can also give you access to LinkedIn Live video, Audio Events, Newsletters and Follow tools.

7.7.1 LinkedIn Live Video

LinkedIn Live currently requires a third party application and integration process so it is not for the faint hearted. That may change in the future. Either way, you will need to be very intentional about promoting the event yourself and be ready to set yourself up for success.

If the LinkedIn Live Event is associated with a LinkedIn Page, it will be retained and visible in the future on the Events tab and people will be able to register after the event and watch the recording. This means that it will have some use to you after the event has occurred and you can re-share the link to the recording as a Post.

LinkedIn Live Events that attract a reasonable level of engagement through the chat facility can allow Hosts to follow up after the event and can potentially be a good source of warm leads.

Most of my clients and students do not have the time or resources to explore this option and most of the LinkedIn Lives I have attended have not had a lot of attendees because they have not been well promoted or because the exact time does not suit every potential attendee.

I personally prefer to create video content that can be found on an as-needs basis when the person is interested in the topic and I incorporate videos in other LinkedIn Posts and Articles because as a general rule, I am time poor and I need one piece of content to provide value more than once over an extended time frame.

However, if your target audience enjoys LinkedIn Lives in your time zone, then you could definitely consider running LinkedIn Lives and to gain the most value, I would probably suggest a reasonably consistent day and time schedule so that your fans can add you to their calendar.

7.7.2 LinkedIn Audio Events

Audio Events require an understanding of running an audio event and the etiquette of being a moderator, being on the audio stage, sticking to an agenda, going on and off mute, and inviting other people in the 'room' to speak by calling for people to raise their hand, managing awkward moments and inappropriate comments as well as using additional technology (like sound effects from your own device) appropriately. At present, they are not recorded.

This is essentially LinkedIn's version of the Clubhouse Social Audio App (or Twitter Spaces). It requires people to attend live which may not suit an international audience and it has limitations in relation to text chatting during the event. as you can only provide a Reaction emoji or direct message other people who are on the screen via LinkedIn Messaging.

As a general rule, there are more people who 'lurk' in Audio Rooms and only listen but do not raise their hand to go on stage. Good Moderators can create a very engaging environment and encourage people to connect with one another or share the latest news that may not have been recorded in a Post or Article (some people do not like writing).

People who are highly on-trend or early-adopters appear to enjoy this environment and highly competent multi-taskers can listen to an Audio Event and complete other tasks at the same time.

A very cool feature in Audio Events via the three dots is the ability to have a chat transcript running which means that people who cannot have the audio sound playing can still 'listen' in (another Universal Design feature).

Audio Events would definitely appeal to people who enjoy radio programs, podcasts and audio content. People who have been a Speaker at an Audio Event may also have it mentioned on their LinkedIn Profile. Once again, most of my clients and students are not ready for the time specific investment involved.

7.7.3 LinkedIn Newsletter

I do recommend the LinkedIn Newsletter feature for genuine content Creators, particularly if you have a lot of Connections as the first edition will be sent to all of your Connections and it will invite them to subscribe.

I am committed to publishing my own LinkedIn Newsletter every month. I publish the content on my own website first, then LinkedIn and then I email it to everyone on my email newsletter mailing list. One piece of content is re-used three times and it includes links to other items I have published during that month. I publish it under my LinkedIn Profile and under my LinkedIn Page. This is the value of re-purposing!

After you have created a LinkedIn Newsletter, every time you go to add a new Article, LinkedIn will assume you are doing another Newsletter, so make sure you choose 'Create an individual article' if you only want to publish an Article. I have made this mistake more than once!

If you would like to see how many Subscribers you have or see your past Newsletters, visit the My Network tab from the Top Menu and then choose Newsletters https://www.linkedin.com/mynetwork/network-manager/newsletters. The top of the list will show you as an Author and your number of Subscribers.

If you are publishing a Newsletter and people choose to Follow you in the future, they will automatically be invited to Subscribe to your Newsletter. This is extremely powerful at increasing the size of your readership and I believe it is potentially a better experience for people who are tired of receiving emails and prefer to receive Notifications within LinkedIn. It also means they won't miss your news if it was only published in the Newsfeed.

You could also go through your list of Subscribers and invite them to Connect with you on LinkedIn as they are clearly already interested in your content.

7.7.4 Follow Tools

The Follow tools section provides a personalized link or code to help you to invite people to follow you online. This link is useful to put on your website so that one click will take them to a screen where all they need to do is Confirm that they would like to Follow you.

Overall, I would say that Creator Mode is probably not relevant for people who are passive users of LinkedIn and do not Post on a regular basis. Please remember though that like most social media platforms, the people who are more active are more likely to attract more opportunities.

If creating content is not really your thing, being an attentive listener by engaging with other people's content can be very worthwhile (Section 10).

7.8 Featured Content

The Featured section allows you to showcase specific Posts, Articles, Links or Media at the beginning of your LinkedIn Profile screen. You do not have to produce your own content here, you can showcase somebody else's work that resonates with your philosophy and approach going forward.

Alternatively, this is a very good place to provide a 'show reel' video where you introduce yourself and your offering (but please don't make it too long). This is particularly useful if you are applying for remote work or you are the main 'face' of your business. A lot of people prefer video to text, so allowing people to 'watch' you on screen as an introduction can be helpful and also prepare you for a video job interview.

I run regular monthly events on LinkedIn so I feature these here as well as a link to subscribe to my LinkedIn Newsletter.

7.9 Experience

For now, I will focus on recording the details of your past working experience. I have chosen to include my entire working history (except the babysitting work I did as a teenager) as I am very proud of the variety of experience I have gained and I would never remember all of the details if I didn't write them down at the time! After all, I have been on LinkedIn since 2003 but started work in 1982.

Likewise, if people don't want to hire me because they think I am too old (ageism) because I have included more than the last 10 years of my experience on my LinkedIn Profile, then I don't want to work for them anyway!

I keep myself up to date by attending up to four events every week and I have done this continuously since completing my university studies in 2000. I sometimes wonder how many other people do the same. Are you committed to continuous and life-long learning? The world is changing so rapidly that in my view, we need to make an effort to stay up to date.

I am also very proud of the work I completed at the beginning of my career and you should be proud of all of your achievements too, even if they are in completely different industries or professions! I have seen a lot of people switch careers and it makes for an interesting back story, one that you do not have to repeat over and over again when connecting with people for the first time.

My ultimate goal is to be found in search results for the type of services I offer right now, but talking about what I have done over many years demonstrates a variety of capabilities and transferable skills and helps me appear in more search results in the first place.

The 'selling' of what I do now comes from the top section of my LinkedIn Profile including my Photo, Headline, About and current Experience sections.

So that means, regardless of my past experience, that my main message is at the top of my LinkedIn Profile (this is also worth remembering if you are considering a change of career or business or want to focus on one dimension of your many dimensions).

If you are creating a new LinkedIn Profile, or updating an existing one, the Experience section will potentially take the most time to complete, especially if you already have several years of work experience, some of which you may have already forgotten. That's okay, just try and do some work each day until you have completed this section. Once it is done, it is done and you don't have to repeat your story every time you meet someone new.

If the information you are adding is more than 10 years old, you could group together some roles (particularly if you have worked in high turnover industries like hospitality). However, if you have worked for some well-respected enterprizes, having their logos on your LinkedIn Profile will add you to more search results and can showcase your experience more effectively for people who absorb new information visually.

Don't worry if you are just starting your career either. If you had one week of work experience at a local business, this can still be added to your LinkedIn Profile and demonstrate that you have some experience in the world of work. If you have moved countries and have a 'job for now,' it is still good to include that you are working locally and gaining some local work experience, even if you are working in a very casual role just to pay the bills. It shows that you have local experience and you are willing to work.

If you have had a significant time break between roles, you can either add in what you were doing between roles or you can consider mentioning a start date and an end date and combine roles between those dates. 'Date Gap Filler' roles can talk about taking a sabbatical, doing research, studying, learning more about life (also known as recovering from an illness), caring for family etc. It is up to you how you decide to record this information.

In my own LinkedIn Profile, I have amalgamated several years after my first job at Westpac Banking Corporation with one 'job' that included a longer time period and a summary of the work and organizations where I worked to 'disguise' my combined roles of parenting, studying and work. Some of the positions listed were very short term – like two days, but the total duration from when I left the bank to when I Founded Newcomers Network was nearly seven years!

For each role you list individually, you can start with the job title followed by keywords you want to be found for with a total of 100 characters. e.g. Project Manager – Commercial Building Construction Development, Design, Planning, Sourcing & Costing. Ideally, these words will also be in your LinkedIn Headline.

Ideally, you will select your Employer from the drop-down field, if they have a Company or School Page on LinkedIn. If it is your own business, you can create a LinkedIn Page at https://www.linkedin.com/company/setup/new.

The format I like to use for each work role is to list Achievements or Impacts first with short bullet points underneath, Tasks second with short bullet points underneath and then provide a Description of the enterprize third with a copied and pasted link to the enterprize website and adding additional media (image, video, website link, document) to add some color and flavor to your LinkedIn Profile.

Achievements and Impacts are discussed in the next section of this book in more significant detail as these can be challenging to write. Achievements and Impacts are usually written in the past tense as they have already been achieved.

I do not like the word 'Responsibilities' because you may be responsible for something but do nothing to make it happen. I much prefer 'Tasks' as it makes it clear that is what you were doing in each role.

Your tasks can be written in the present tense, even if they are in past roles. This makes your content appear more up to date and present-focused.

Tasks outline the specific details of what you complete in each role. You may be surprised at the long list of tasks you have completed. Don't underestimate the value of going into extensive detail. A junior employee may feel that all they do are three menial and repetitive tasks, but they may have also completed on-the-job and online training, abided by occupational health and safety guidelines, participated in team meetings and so much more.

The Description of the enterprize can be written in third person narrative unless it is your own enterprize that you have established and then it can be written in first person narrative.

The description of the organization usually starts with 'Established in XXXX, XYZ organization provides ABC goods and services to DEF customers locally and internationally.' Finding the year an enterprize was established can be tricky but will hopefully be on either their website or their LinkedIn Page or maybe even Wikipedia. If you are currently working for the organization, you could also include your work email address and phone number as well as the website link.

All of the content for each role needs to be keyword driven and related to both your actual experience and the preferences you have moving forward (without lying or over-stating anything along the way). As I mentioned in the About section, please list the most important and aligned items for your values, purpose, goals and objectives first. You can shuffle these items in a different order for a résumé or curriculum vitae that you submit for a specific job role.

The text in the description box for each role you have had in the Experience section would appear like this:

Achievements (or Impacts)
> achievement a
> achievement b
> achievement c, etc

Tasks
> task a
> task b
> task c, etc

Description
Established in 2001, XYZ organization provides ABC goods and services to DEF customers locally and internationally.

https://xyzorganization.com
sellson@xyzorganization.com
+61 402 333 444

+ Media Upload or Link + Media Upload or Link

Remember that the shorter the bullet points are, the quicker and easier they are to read, process, find and remember. Ideally, less than five words in each bullet point, starting with lower case letters unless it is a name.

If possible, please include an Experience item in your LinkedIn Profile that covers the present date. I believe a lot of recruiters and decision-makers prefer to hire someone who is already working and the search algorithm appears to have a preference for someone who is currently in a role related to their search query.

You do not need to lie – and you never should. But you can say that you are doing 'Career Research – Keyword, Keyword, Keyword etc.' For example, if you are not working right now, your Job Title could be 'Career Research – Project Manager – Commercial Building Construction

Development, Design, Planning.' You can list your Employer as 'Various" and your Start Date as the date when you left your previous role.

In the Description field, you can focus on the skills and keywords related to the type of work you would like to secure in the future and even list a range of preferred Tasks. Once a viewer reads this content, they will be able to see that you are currently available and that you are proactive in your approach. More importantly, you are more likely to appear in search results.

Alternatively, if you have been running your own enterprize/s, you may like to provide different details in the Description field and include details of your products, services and where people can find you online, including links to your other social media. It is up to you. However, once again, the more primary and secondary keywords you can include in the Description field, the more search results you can attract!

Please don't overdo it on the additional media items. One client added virtually every product available in his employer's sales catalogue and all of a sudden, he looked like a 'try hard' and 'desperate' with so much product information on his LinkedIn Profile. My recommendation is two media items for each position and my favorites would be a relevant video and a website link with a good quality image that is automatically selected when you add the link.

There is room for you to tailor some of the text on the screen when you add the additional media or links, so if appropriate, you may like to tweak this content for your values, purpose, goals and objectives.

7.9.1 Achievements Or Impacts

Sadly, a lot of people I have worked with do not believe they have achieved very much in their working life and they are very uncomfortable sharing their achievements and impacts online. Ironically, when I ask them what they have done and help them put it in writing, they suddenly realize they have a lot to offer! Some people even call it 'Imposter Syndrome.'

If you find this process difficult, you may like to team up with a Career Specialist, coach, mentor or trusted colleague or friend. Perhaps you can help write the content for a friend and they can help write the content for you.

Adding your achievements or impacts to your LinkedIn Profile can help you:

- Be recognized within the enterprize.
- Secure a promotion or an aligned offer.

- Be respected by your fellow colleagues and competitors.

- Recall them in the future as you may forget some of them.

Writing your achievements or impacts on your LinkedIn Profile can also be a great strategy for sharing your 'news' without boasting or broadcasting it in the Newsfeed.

I like to define an Achievement as anything you have done particularly well or anything over and above what you were originally asked to complete.

For example, you may have been asked to achieve X within six months but you achieved it within three months. You may have been selected to do X, seconded to do Y or invited to do Z but these were all over and above your initial task list when you started in the role. You could have been asked to mentor, coach or train other team members.

You may have been recognized by fellow workers, peers, managers, customers, clients or stakeholders for your work and perhaps even received formal recognition for your efforts (honors, awards, certificates etc).

You may have found better ways to complete your existing tasks and found a way to save time, money or effort. You may have collaborated effectively with other employees and provided recommendations for the future.

To identify your achievements, run through the list of tasks you are required to do for each role and reflect on what you did well and what you did in addition to the original job description or project brief.

Here are some of the words that can be used to start the description of each achievement:

- achieved
- assisted
- awarded
- coached
- created
- collaborated
- conducted

- delegated
- delivered
- developed
- encouraged
- established
- expanded
- focused
- hosted
- implemented
- initiated
- instigated
- invited
- learned
- managed
- mentored
- outsourced
- part of
- presented
- proactively
- promoted
- provided
- received
- recognized
- recommended
- re-designed

- referred
- regularly
- represented
- researched
- reviewed
- seconded
- secured
- selected
- shared
- solved
- started
- trained
- transferred

You may be able to think of others. Try and describe your Achievements in a way that the viewer of your LinkedIn Profile understands the value of your contribution. In some cases, you may need to list a role twice so that you can fill in all the detail because you run out of characters in the first Description box. Remember to still use the same dates.

Please do NOT include any of the following in your list of achievements:

- Anything of a commercially sensitive nature. It is not appropriate to name clients (unless you have their written permission), specific numbers (percentages may be okay) or anything that gives away information that is identifiable, unsuitable for public consumption or could be used by a competitor to gain advantage.

- Saying 'I' this and 'I' that and 'I' something else. It can look like bragging. Simply state what happened.

- Superfluous adjectives. Just state facts.

An Impact goes into more detail about the consequences of your Achievements. You can describe the non-sensitive results, the feedback you received and the consequence of your actions.

Achievements or Impacts can be added in the Description box for your Experience items, but also in your Voluntary Experience items and in your Honors and Awards. It may also be appropriate to add them in the Education or Publications sections too, depending on the nature of the Achievement or Impact.

Achievements or Impacts can be even more important than the Tasks you have completed. They are an example of what you have done over and above what you were originally asked to do and can provide insights as to what you can do in the future. Remember to include as many of your aligned keywords as possible.

Writing these achievements down can also help you prepare for behavioral interview questions where you are invited to provide examples of what you have done in different situations and then what happened as a result.

7.9.2 Tasks

Hopefully you will have a list of the Tasks you have completed from your previous roles in the form of individual job descriptions that you can add to your LinkedIn Profile, although I suspect you may no longer have access to all of these or the job may have changed over time from when you first accepted the position and the date the position ended.

The priority Tasks that you need to list on your LinkedIn Profile are those that are most aligned with what you want to achieve in the immediate and longer term future. Hopefully they also have relevant keywords. Remember that you must not lie but you can massage the message and you can focus on your transferable skills, knowledge and networks. Your experiences have made you who you are and they are all interesting. No time is ever wasted and it is never too late (well it is too late for me to be a brain surgeon but I still have quite a lot of other choices I can make).

If you are planning a change of career, you may choose to focus on the more generic transferable skills tasks first rather than the very specific technical tasks. If your role involved some industry specific jargon, you may like to re-word those tasks in terminology that someone outside the industry would understand. Alternatively, if you want to specialize in that industry, the more of those industry-specific words you can include, the better and you would list them first.

Anyone who has had a long history in one area may find it difficult to convince viewers of their LinkedIn Profile that they can transition into another area without careful massaging of the message. Therefore, it is important to demonstrate in a list of Tasks any details of liaison with people or tasks outside of that main area. This is especially important for people who have spent many years in one area like government, education or the military or in one industry or profession. People outside of that area may make assumptions about your ability to transfer your skills to a different environment. You need to show what you can transfer across.

You can incorporate information about your side projects, side hustles, voluntary experience and other interests as skills learnt in these areas can also be applied to a professional area of work. For example, someone who has a background in the corporate world but spends a lot of time in community based sport could list one range of Tasks in the Experience section with their corporate role and another range of Tasks in the Voluntary Experience section with their community based sport role.

If there is enough room in the individual Description sections for either Experience or Voluntary Experience to list all of your Achievements or Impacts and all of your Tasks for each role, I encourage you to do so.

When you prepare a résumé or curriculum vitae for a specific job or work, you can then hand pick the Achievements and Tasks to include that align with the position you are applying for and then you won't need to include everything you have mentioned on your LinkedIn Profile. Remember that the more content you have online, the more likely you are to appear in aligned search engine results. Likewise, some Applicant Tracking Systems (ATS) will only use the content in your résumé or curriculum vitae so make sure all of your keywords are included in that document (and not just in the cover letter or email message accompanying your job application).

Having the one source of truth on your LinkedIn Profile also makes life a lot easier because you won't need to scroll through multiple different résumés or curriculum vitaes of past job applications to collect different excerpts relevant for each role.

I recommend that you have one full length résumé that lists everything and then each time you apply for a role, you save the document with a new file name date-backwards-your-name-job-title-company-name and you edit it accordingly, shuffling items into the most logical order and removing details that are unnecessary. When you look at the final saved filename, you can see exactly which résumé you sent for which role at which organization. I am not so worried about length, but I do insist that the content be Applicant Tracking System ATS friendly and scan friendly for skim readers and small screens. I recommend 11 point font for the majority of the text and no text boxes or fancy formatting as this cannot be 'read' by some Applicant Tracking Systems.

7.9.3 Add Career Break

An alternative when you go to add a Position to your LinkedIn Profile in the Experience section is the option to select a 'Career Break' instead. The current options include Bereavement, Career transition, Caregiving, Full-time parenting, Gap year, Layoff/position eliminated, Health and well-being, Personal goal pursuit, Professional development, Relocation, Retirement, Travel, and Voluntary Work.

I totally agree with the concept that we should all be able to take some time out of our professional lives to do other things and this section enables you to choose an option that applies to you.

However, it only allows you to choose one type of Career Break, the Location, the Dates and a Description.

It doesn't give you a Job Title or an Employer field and as far as I can tell, the Algorithm uses the Job Title field as a way to find you in Search Results.

I have also found that for most of my clients and students, whilst they may be taking a break, they are doing more than one thing during that time and I do not want anyone to suffer from some form of discrimination by declaring this information publicly.

I encourage you to look at these options for a bit of self-validation but for you to list any time (date gaps) between roles in a more descriptive way by treating it as an Experience with a title and leave the Employer section as 'Various' but do not choose 'Various' from the drop-down box.

This is particularly helpful if you still include your Keywords in the Job Title field. For example, you may have been on Sabbatical but you could have also been Writing and Studying X Topic and Travelling. In the Description box, you could then go into a lot more detail and even use the same formula of Achievements, Tasks and Description if it is relevant.

After my full time banking career, I completed many different roles over the next seven years and because they are from a 'long time ago,' I have grouped them in to one role with one set of dates and provided more specific information in the Description box. This also enabled me to cover some date gaps when I was actively parenting my young children, studying part time, volunteering and only doing occasional paid work.

7.10 Education

This is one of my favorite LinkedIn Profile sections. You can add formal qualifications from Secondary School, Tertiary Education, Training Organizations, Universities and Professional Associations, even if you didn't complete the formal qualification (just include the subjects you did complete so that you can still be a part of the School's alumni on LinkedIn).

You can also add micro-credentials that you have completed more recently as well as formal accreditation or certification programs from professional associations. It is even better if those associations have a School Page on LinkedIn so that their logos can appear next to the respective accreditations or certifications you have completed (remember to select it from the drop-down box if it is available).

Most people do not complete the Description field within the Education section and this is where I recommend that you:

- Describe the institution (again, Established in XXXX, ABC University is a research based university focused on the principles of A, B and C with campuses in Location 1, Location 2 and Location 3).
- Include the Subjects you completed listed in alphabetical order (no need to include the grades for each).
- Include the Topics you completed if the keywords of those topics are important for your values, purpose, goals and objectives.
- Include the Qualification you secured and the Certificate Number if applicable.
- Include a URL website link to the educational facility so that these details can be confirmed directly with the School if required.

Why should you include topics? Well, if your Subjects included Topics that are significant keywords for you, then having those keywords in your Education section will increase your chances of appearing in search results.

For example, I completed a subject called Business Ethics. If I wanted to secure a board member position, I would need to understand governance, risk and compliance (GRC) and all of these topics were discussed in this subject. These are fantastic keywords to have in my Education section and would help me appear in search results if I listed them as Topics even though they were not Subjects of my University course.

You can add Media as well (either an Upload or Link). Some people choose to add a copy of their Certificate of Completion or Academic Transcript. This can look a little untidy, so I have chosen to link to a video of the educational facility. For clients, I sometimes link to the course description for more information for the viewer. Overall, it would appear like this:

Established in XXXX, ABC University is a research based university focused on the principles of A, B and C with campuses in Location 1, Location 2 and Location 3.

Subjects Completed
> Subject a

> Subject b
> Subject c, etc

Topics Included
> Topic a
> Topic b
> Topic c, etc

https://abcuniversity.edu + Media Upload or Link

The four line 'hamburger' toggle on the side of your screen can be used to click and drag the order of your Education so that you can put the study that is most relevant or recognized for your goals at the top of the list.

I have chosen to include my Secondary Education as I am proud of the schools where I studied. You may like to have a look at the websites of the various places where you have studied and find out what they offer for alumni (including your secondary school).

Now could be a good time to reconnect with your study friends but also learn more about what is happening there now and what services, support and opportunities they provide for alumni. You may like to offer your own philanthropic, mentoring or guest speaking support and join their LinkedIn Group if they have one https://www.linkedin.com/search/results/groups.

Most secondary schools have a requirement that you cannot connect with your teachers or lecturers until two years after your study at that school has been completed. If it has been longer than two years, you may like to reconnect with your favorite teachers.

Don't forget that you can complete online courses through LinkedIn Learning. These are often called 'Micro Credentials' and once completed, they can be added to your LinkedIn Profile at the press of a button in the Licenses and Certifications section. Some other recent short courses related to your current and future goals could also be added in the Education section as the Courses section only provides the name of the Course whereas the Education section allows you to go into a lot more detail. If this is important for your current values, purpose, goals and objectives, it may be worth the time to provide more detail in the Education section.

7.11 Licenses And Certifications

This section can be used for listing licenses, certifications and professional memberships (because many professional associations require you to be at a certain skill level to secure membership). Rather than just mentioning the name of your license, certification or membership, I encourage you to add in the name of the governing body as well in the Name field so that it 'stands out' on your LinkedIn Profile e.g. Professional Member – XYZ Association.

Make sure that you choose the name of the governing body from the drop-down box so that the logo from their LinkedIn Page appears on your LinkedIn Profile. If you have a Member number you can include it in the Credential ID, to give you more credibility, although for privacy reasons, if you don't feel comfortable including this information, you could copy and paste the website URL in both this field and the Credential URL field.

I have also listed Associate Memberships as well as full Professional Memberships. I believe it is important to support your profession and/or industry by joining the representative body. It keeps you informed, encourages you to maintain high levels of ongoing professional development, promotes certification and after many years, you may secure fellowship or free lifetime membership.

I have also chosen to leave previous memberships on my LinkedIn Profile. Just because I no longer pay the fee, it doesn't mean I should remove it from my LinkedIn Profile. Once again, the logo on your LinkedIn Profile provides important brand recognition, especially if you have been a member of an association for many years.

Many professional associations offer discounted or free memberships to students so it is a good idea to join the association whilst you are still studying and pay the discounted rate for the first year rather than the full professional rate immediately after graduating.

Some of my best work experiences have been related to active membership and support of various professional associations. I love the opportunity to learn from fellow members at events and conferences and glean the latest insights by serving on committees, councils and boards.

This section is automatically sorted in descending start date order. Up to 50 completed LinkedIn Learning Courses can be automatically added to this section. I also recommend adding any Organizations mentioned here in the Organizations section.

7.12 Volunteer Experience

Voluntary and Pro Bono work has played a key part in my personal and professional development and growth and I believe everyone should allow time in their life to provide some sort of voluntary service, ideally aligned with their values, strengths and context as well as their values, purpose, goals and objectives.

Local community activity is where you are probably most likely to gain the most social benefit, but with a connected planet, you can consider global voluntary opportunities as well.

As a former recruiter, I can assure you that many decision-makers will look at this section of your LinkedIn Profile with great interest.

You don't need to be focused solely on charity or welfare experiences either. My roles have changed over the years according to my work interests, capabilities and personal lifestyle. I have chosen to align the professional experiences with my overall work goals.

One of the best voluntary experiences I had was taking teenagers out sailing on Sydney Harbor for two weeks during the Australian Scouts Jamboree. I was the only skipper who did not capsize the boat during that time in variable wind conditions and with inexperienced crew!

On the other end of the scale, I have provided professional speaking and writing services to local and international organizations and universities. I love the idea of being able to pass on my experience to people from all walks of life at different ages and stages.

The Voluntary Experience section can be completed in the same format as the Experience section (Section 7.9) where you include your Achievements or Impacts, Tasks and Description of the Organization. Unfortunately you cannot add in Media here, so I encourage you to make the text as interesting and visually descriptive as possible.

The four line 'hamburger' on the side of your screen can be used to click and drag the order of your Volunteer Experience so that you can put the Volunteer Experience that is most relevant or recognized for your values, purpose, goals and objectives at the top of the list.

7.13 Skills And Endorsements

I encourage you to select Skills that match your keywords and are hopefully within the list of skills in the LinkedIn database (and can be chosen from the drop-down field as you start typing them).

You can select three skills to Pin to the top of the list as 'Top Skills' and these will be visible at all times. You can have a maximum of 50 skills in total. If you want to focus your work in some specific areas, I would suggest you pick a maximum of 20 skills. I am much more of a generalist, so I have chosen the maximum number of 50 skills. If you have a skill that is not listed, I encourage you to write each word with a capital letter at the beginning to keep the look and feel of your list of Skills consistent.

Within the Skills listing, LinkedIn allows you to sort them into your order of listed preference and also align your Skills with items in your Experience, Education, Licenses and Certifications, Volunteering, Publications, Courses, Projects, Honors & Awards and Organizations sections on your LinkedIn Profile.

I recommend that you aim to have at least 20 endorsements from people in your network for each of your Top Three Skills that are Pinned and visible at all times.

You may need to invite your Connections to do this for you with a personal message and likewise, you may choose to endorse Connections in your network for some of their Skills (it will also send them a Notification which is a good way to reconnect with people you know). As far as I can tell, a higher weighting is given to your Skills votes if you are endorsed by people you work with or have studied with or who have also received multiple endorsements for the same Skill.

If you choose to Endorse a Skill for one of your Connections, you will be invited to describe how good they are at that Skill (Good, Very Good or Highly Skilled) and your Relationship to that person (Worked directly on the same team or project, Managed Person directly, Reported directly to Person, Worked together indirectly, Heard about Person's skill from others, None of the above). This is only a LinkedIn record and is not available publicly.

When Endorsements first appeared on LinkedIn, many people thought they were a waste of time and unlikely to be accurate. However, over time, the enthusiasm to endorse people for the sole purpose of attracting their attention via a Notification has slowed down.

If you assume that at least 60% of the Endorsements are accurate, you will be able to gain a general idea about someone's capabilities.

If you have key clients, stakeholders, network Connections and colleagues that are good at what they do, I encourage you to acknowledge their Skills by endorsing them, or better still, if you have seen them in action, write them a Recommendation! It is one of the most valuable engagement tools.

There is also a Skills Assessment Quiz that allows you to answer 15 multiple choice questions and if you score in the top 30%, you can earn a Skill Badge. At present, most of the quizzes are for very technical information technology related skills. If you want to be recognized for these skills, I would recommend that you 'earn' your Skills Badges, so it is a good idea to check the list every six months and see if you can answer those 15 questions.

7.14 Recommendations

Did you know that a written Recommendation could be used in a court of law? I don't want that to scare you into not writing Recommendations, but I would like to remind you that it is important to be completely honest when you write a Recommendation.

The example I often use in my training sessions is writing a Recommendation for a Project Manager. Let's assume that this Project Manager was able to make sure that project timelines and budgets were always met. However, in the process, they may have been overly directive in their approach and this may have upset several members of the project team. It would be inappropriate to suggest that this person is an outstanding Project Manager as their people leadership skills appear to be lacking.

The Recommendation could include the details of their ability to maintain timelines and budgets, but it would not be a good idea to say that they were an outstanding Project Manager. Likewise, if you think about what you would be prepared to say in court, you could confidently say they met timelines and budgets but you could not confidently say that they were an outstanding Project Manager.

The style guide I use for Recommendations is to start by mentioning how I met the person, then explain the capabilities I witnessed for myself and then give them my best wishes for the future and end with my name (in the text area).

It would appear like this:

I first met Alex J Rogers in my role as the Convenor for the International Human Resources Management Network Group of the Australian Human Resources Institute (AHRI). Alex joined the committee as a member of AHRI with a background in global mobility and immigration. Alex attended meetings on a regular basis, provided excellent insights into their field of experience and willingly accepted responsibility for coordinating the speakers and venues for several professional development functions. Alex arrived at our events early and welcomed people arriving for the first time as well as regular members and speakers. Alex has made a valuable contribution to the IHRM Network Group and I would like to wish Alex all the best in the future. Sue Ellson :).

As you can see here, I have not talked about Alex's global mobility and immigration expertise, because I have not witnessed those skills. I still included those words because I am aware that they are keywords for Alex and they are relevant in terms of the role with the Group. I talked about what I have observed in specific visual detail so that people reading this Recommendation would understand that Alex is both capable and thoughtful in their approach. I have included my name at the end as an additional reminder that I am the person who has written the Recommendation for Alex. I have also added a 'smiley face' in text which is something I personally do on a regular basis.

In the statistics collecting process earlier (Section 4.3), I mentioned the importance of having a similar number of Recommendations both given and received and to have a minimum of six of each. If you give more than you receive or receive more than you give, this can create a sense of imbalance so I do my best to keep the numbers relatively even.

I believe it is important to acknowledge other people. If you choose to Recommend someone who attracts a lot of views to their LinkedIn Profile, you could attract additional views to your LinkedIn Profile and you could consider this to be a strategic move, particularly if they have been recognized for similar Skills and they have similar keywords in their LinkedIn Profile. On the other hand, it is just as important to recognize your colleagues, clients and stakeholders for their efforts, even if they do not attract as many viewers to their LinkedIn Profile.

Whilst most people are happy to build the size of their network on LinkedIn, it seems that a lot of people on LinkedIn do not write Recommendations. I believe it is important to acknowledge a person's efforts or contribution and I can assure you, most people enjoy receiving written Recommendations. If you are asked to provide a Recommendation, particularly from someone you have never met in person, you can choose whether or not you would like to do so. The model above allows you to only comment on what you have observed online or in person.

For example, I have had some people, who I have only met once or twice, ask me for a Recommendation. I cannot possibly ascertain their overall level of competence in two meetings, but I can explain what I have observed. One presenter at a workshop I attended was so outstanding that I wrote a Recommendation immediately afterwards. Whilst I realize that this is rare, in my view, their performance deserved instant recognition.

Please remember that before a Recommendation can appear on a LinkedIn Profile, the recipient can decide whether or not to publish it. If you think this is your chance to 'write them a bad review' they may choose not to publish it. They also need to be a First Level Connection for you to be able to write a Recommendation.

I also believe that a lot of people don't write Recommendations because they don't know what to say. They also don't like to ask for Recommendations either. So, if you have decided that you need to ask a few people you are connected to for a Recommendation, I encourage you to provide them with some ideas on what to include in the Recommendation.

Your request via a direct message on LinkedIn could go something like this. "Hi George. I have been updating my LinkedIn Profile recently as I am interested in securing a new role in the XYZ industry. As we have worked together in the past, I was wondering if you would be able to write a Recommendation for me on LinkedIn that focuses on my skills in the area of A, B and C. To do this, simply visit my LinkedIn Profile at https://www.linkedin.com/in/georgepopodopoulos and click on 'More' and choose 'Recommend.' Thanks in advance, Sue."

Alternatively, you could visit George's LinkedIn Profile and click on 'More' and then choose 'Request a Recommendation' and follow the prompts and provide the message just before you press 'Send.'

7.15 Organizations

This is a section where you can list your involvement in Organizations, whether you were a member or played a more minor role. This section asks you to choose which work Experience or Education the role is associated with.

Once again, I find that a lot of people do not provide a lot of detail in this section, so I encourage you to provide URL links to the Organization, particularly if you have a Profile Page on their website. You can also include an additional description that could be helpful to the viewer of your LinkedIn Profile.

For me, this section aligns once again with the Licenses and Certifications section and items in this section are listed in the order they were entered in to LinkedIn (another good reason to collect your information before filling in your LinkedIn Profile).

You can list a professional membership in both the Licenses and Certifications section as well as the Organizations section.

7.16 Honors And Awards

Anything from 'Employee of the Month' to a knighthood can be included. The goal here is to ensure that most sections of your LinkedIn Profile have some content and if you are at the very early stages of your working life, 'Employee of the Month' could be a good place to start. If this occurs 36 times, that could be classified as a bit of overkill and be re-worded by recording the Honor once and include the 36 months in the Description field.

This section will also ask you to choose which work Experience or Education the Honor or Award is associated with and it provides a Description field where you can include the URL and specific details of the Honor or Award.

I encourage you to feel pleased with any formal recognition you have received for your efforts, regardless of how credible the Honor or Award may feel to you. If you are a student and you received a school subject award, like the 'LL Jones Geography Award,' it would be a good idea to explain the nature of the award. For example, 'The most outstanding geography project for a Year 9 student during the school year.'

If you are in a business or enterprize, I encourage you to enter awards as you can say you have been an entrant, a finalist or a winner depending on the results. Just being an entrant is an achievement. The process of completing an application can be an eye-opening learning experience in itself and can give you guidance and ideas on how you can improve your enterprize in the future. Most awards have a selection criteria so even meeting this criteria is an achievement.

7.17 Publications

This section allows you to add in articles, journals, magazines, books, apps, podcasts etc – in fact anything classified as published. If you have a co-author and are connected to them on LinkedIn, you can also add them as a co-author.

If you are at the early stages of your work life, try and get something published so you can fill in this section! If you are a bit further down the track, you may choose to be more selective about the Publications you mention here and provide a more comprehensive list on your own website.

Again, I invite you to include URL links because in this section, they will be clickable.

7.18 Languages

Firstly, you need to include your native Language on your LinkedIn Profile. That is why I say this is the easiest section to complete on your LinkedIn Profile.

There is a long held belief that if you can speak more than one language, you will have more intellectual capabilities than a person who can only speak one language, so I encourage you to mention all of the languages you have ever used, even if you only have a very basic level of ability to use the language.

This includes languages you have studied at school or after school. I could suggest that because I studied French at school for five years, I potentially know some Spanish and Italian, but that is going a bit too far!

LinkedIn also allows you to include your level of competency. So although I studied French at school for five years, I have chosen the Elementary Proficiency option.

Languages are listed on your LinkedIn Profile in alphabetical order. Chinese written language can be used to speak Mandarin or Cantonese. LinkedIn allows you to add Chinese, but depending on which Asian country you are living or working in, it may be helpful to add 'Mandarin' or 'Cantonese' as well in the Languages section, even though they are not choices currently available on the drop-down list. This visual cue could be very helpful for decision-makers reading your LinkedIn Profile or finding you via a Google Advanced Search.

This section is only about your Language competency. If you want to prepare a LinkedIn Profile in another language you can do so at https://www.linkedin.com/in/YOURURL/edit/secondary-language. This is particularly helpful if you are living in a foreign country but regularly provide services or business to a previous home country.

If you would like the content on your screen as you use LinkedIn translated into another language, you can adjust this at https://www.linkedin.com/psettings/select-language-for-translation.

7.19 Projects

In my view, the Projects section is one of the most under-utilized sections of a LinkedIn Profile. If you are going to be involved in a job interview, you will often be asked behavioral questions that start with a statement like "Tell me about a time when." If you have described some Projects on your LinkedIn Profile, you may have the story partly prepared and ready to share.

Once again, please do not include anything of a commercially sensitive nature and percentages are preferable to actual numbers or currency amounts.

If you are describing a typical work-based project, you may like to include the title of the Project, a description of the Project, any challenges you overcame, results and feedback received as well as future expected outcomes or impacts.

If you are not sure which projects to include of the many you have completed, you may like to choose one that has a professional skills focus, another with a technical skills focus and another with a personal skills focus.

For example, a Productivity Improvement Project where you analyzed a situation and designed and implemented new procedures, a Software Development Upgrade where you had to do the hands on coding and editing and a Change Transformation Project where you had to bring about significant cultural change through people management. By showcasing three different types of projects, you can reveal a range of your skills, competencies and results.

Remembering projects years after they have been completed can also be difficult. Alternatively, if most of your work is project based, you may still want to include a lot of this information in the Experience section. As I work for so many different clients on a project or gig basis, I have provided links to where you can learn more about my work.

However, as I have said many times before, the key is making sure that most sections of your LinkedIn Profile have some details entered so that your LinkedIn Profile can be classified as 'complete' and you can attract more appearances in aligned search results. If you don't tell, you can't sell.

7.20 Courses

This is a relatively easy section to complete as there are only three fields, Course Name, Number and Associated With (again, Experience or Education). This is why I prefer to mention anything notable and specifically relevant to my values, purpose, goals and objectives in the Education section.

For example, if I did a short half day course but it was at a prestigious university or association that has a School Page on LinkedIn, then I would become a part of their alumni by listing it in my Education section but I would not have the opportunity to provide this information if it was in my Courses section.

However, this is not a reason to leave the Courses section blank! I could add a lot of courses in this section, but I have chosen to only highlight the most relevant and I have added a statement about attending up to four events every week in the About section to demonstrate my commitment to continuous learning (which I believe should average at least 10% of my working hours and includes reading, events, courses, audio and video content etc).

7.21 Test Score

If there is a specific Test that applies to your career or business, then this section allows you to showcase the Title, what it is associated with (Experience or Education), your Score, the Test Date and the Description. For other people, it could be a place to showcase some written reviews, specific feedback or links to online recommendations or awards.

Naturally, there will be many people who may be suspicious of your results so you still need to keep a written record of your results and provide it on request. I rarely see this field completed and I have used it quite creatively for different clients. I don't see it as being a major component of your LinkedIn Profile but I do believe it provides some interesting contextual background.

7.22 Patent

This section will request the Title of the Patent, the location of the Office where your patent has been lodged, the Patent or Application Number, Status (Issued or Pending), URL and Description.

If you don't have a patent, you simply can't fill this one in, so you have my full permission to leave this section blank!

For privacy and approval reasons, you may prefer not to make this public until the Patent has been issued.

7.23 Interests

When you select Influencers, Companies and Schools to follow and Groups to join, they will automatically appear in the Interests section of your LinkedIn Profile and you will also encourage LinkedIn to include their content in your Newsfeed and Notifications.

7.24 Causes You Care About

There are various Causes that are listed here and you simply tick the boxes of the Causes that are important to you. The current list includes:

- Animal Welfare
- Arts and Culture
- Children
- Civil Rights and Social Action
- Disaster and Humanitarian Relief
- Economic Empowerment
- Education
- Environment
- Health
- Human Rights
- Politics
- Poverty Alleviation
- Science and Technology
- Social Services
- Veteran Support

7.25 LinkedIn App - Profile Picture Video, Photo Or Frame

At present, you can add a video 'behind' your Profile Picture via the LinkedIn App on your mobile device.

When you are in the LinkedIn App, click on the circle and it will allow you to View or Edit your Photo and/or Video or alternatively add a Frame around your Profile Picture.

You can either take a Photo or add one from your Phone. You can choose to make your Photo visible to Anyone, All LinkedIn Users, Your Network (up to three degrees) or 1st Degree Connections only. I believe the Photo should be visible to everyone.

When you first open the Video screen, you will see a quotation mark with the word 'Prompts' which will give you some ideas on questions you could answer in your Video like 'Who are you and what do you do for work?' or 'What are you known for?'

Your video can be between three and 30 seconds long. You can also include an @Mention, Clock, Sticker, Text and Resize the Video.

When you go to add a Video, you can either record it directly (in Portrait Mode) or choose a Video from your device. There is a Preview setting which will automatically play the video on mute when people view your Profile that you can turn on. You can also Send this video in a Message on LinkedIn.

After the Video has been uploaded, you can see how many people have viewed your video and/or replace it. When you are back on the Desktop version of LinkedIn, you can upload a .srt file with captions to appear on your LinkedIn Video (remember that you can create a .srt file by uploading your video to YouTube). Once you have uploaded the captions, you cannot change them.

The Frame options are currently None, Open to Work and Hiring. As mentioned previously, I am not a fan of the Open to Work Frame as I feel as if it makes you look desperate.

7.26 LinkedIn App - Audio Pronunciation Of Your Name

The editing pen that allows you to edit your name on LinkedIn will also give you access to the screen that allows you to add a 10 second audio pronunciation of your Name.

This can be very helpful for people on LinkedIn with a name pronunciation that is not familiar to the viewer but it can also be used to include a very brief summary of the value you offer. It is ideal for people who don't like being on camera too! Another great Universal

Design feature. I mention both my name and my current 'label' from my Headline.

7.27 LinkedIn App - Featured Website Link

Descriptive Text and a Link can be featured just beneath your Location and before the line where you can see the number of Followers you have on your LinkedIn Profile.

Once this has been added on a Mobile Device it can be edited on any device. Please copy/paste your link in and use up to 30 characters to describe the nature of your link. This is one of the most important places to add a link on your LinkedIn Profile because it is highly visible and is 'above the fold' - the screen area that is instantly visible without scrolling down.

As I have said several times before, please, please, please complete your own LinkedIn Profile if you want to gain maximum value from the LinkedIn platform.

7.28 LinkedIn App - Scan Code

When you are out and about with the LinkedIn App on your mobile device, you can click the Search Box and then click on the icon on the top right hand side and you will have the option to share your LinkedIn Profile QR Code and turn on your LinkedIn App mobile device camera access.

When you scan another person's QR code, please click the three dots next to the blue Connect or Follow button and choose 'Personalize Invite' and type up a brief message to indicate where you met them so when they receive the electronic invitation, they will remember where they met you and have a record of that interaction.

When you return to your laptop or desktop, you can click on 'My Network' and see your most recent Connections and send a 'thank you for connecting' follow up message.

8. Company, Showcase Or School LinkedIn Pages

If you have your own enterprize or even work for yourself, you can create a LinkedIn Page from the Work Menu drop-down box or go to https://www.linkedin.com/company/setup/new. Just like a Personal LinkedIn Profile, there is a variety of information that can be included.

When you first select this option, you will be asked if you are creating a Small Business, Medium to Large Business, Showcase Page or Educational Institution Page (School).

In the past, a Post in the Newsfeed shared via a personal LinkedIn Profile has had a lot more exposure than a Post shared by a Company, Showcase or School Page. However, that is starting to change and Administrators of Pages are being encouraged to Post twice a week.

In recent times, there has also been a steady increase in the number of features and analytics available for Administrators of LinkedIn Pages.

Firstly, I will talk about solopreneurs. It may not seem 'necessary' to create a LinkedIn Page if you are a business of one person or one person plus a few contractors. However, I have managed to generate quite a lot of interest for my own LinkedIn Page, even though I am the only official Employee and I now have a good number of Followers. It also means that a logo appears in the Experience section of my LinkedIn Profile as I can choose my own LinkedIn Page as my 'Employer' from the drop-down box.

What I particularly like about a LinkedIn Page is that it brings all of the content you have published in an archive together in one place, which makes it very worthwhile from a due diligence perspective (when someone is checking you or your LinkedIn Page). Even so, without a direct link to a Post, you will still only see the last 12 months of Posts.

If you are thinking about selling your enterprize at some point in the future as part of your succession planning, building a digital asset under the business name could increase the sale value of the enterprize. It also allows the new owner to maintain existing Follower relationships rather than start from scratch and ensures that the enterprize can live longer than the original founder.

If you have multiple enterprizes or side hustles, you could create a Page for each one so that the content aligned with each can be shared on the Page rather than your Personal LinkedIn Profile so that you can keep the different content in its own channel.

Showcase Pages are a sub-page of a main LinkedIn Page and are designed to showcase a brand, business unit or organization initiative. They are intended to develop a long-term relationship with a specific audience and have been around for many years. Nowadays, I find most organizations prefer to manage just one LinkedIn Page and perhaps a Group if they want to have ongoing conversations with a specific audience.

School Pages are nearly always automatically approved for well-recognized Schools, Colleges and Universities. However, I encourage professional associations and registered training organizations to also apply for a School Page (which can also act as a Company Page for the Experience section so that staff can use the School Page in their Experience section).

The main benefit of a School Page is that when students select the School in the Education section of their LinkedIn Profile, the School logo can appear on their LinkedIn Profile and the School can automatically keep track of the school alumni via the Alumni feature on the School Page.

For convenience, I will now use the term 'LinkedIn Page' rather than Company Page, Showcase Page or School Page.'

8.1 LinkedIn Page Details

There are some fundamental first steps for LinkedIn Pages (More specific details in Section 13.1). You need to make sure that if a viewer is looking at your LinkedIn Page for the first time, they can understand exactly what you do and how you operate. After all, this is a part of your brand and you want it to be consistent with your other brand messaging.

- **Complete all of the sections** and include as many primary and secondary keywords as possible. Bullet points can be visually scan friendly for viewers using a phone, tablet, laptop or desktop computer and be easier to remember or locate. A narrative can help describe the culture of an enterprize. You can include a call to action in the Description and the type of Call to Action button you would like as well (Contact Us, Learn More, Register, Sign Up or Visit Website).

  The Overview section allows you to add in multiple classifications and 20 Specialties, so make use of all of these as well.

  The Workplace Module can be turned on if you have employees and offer different workstyles including On-site, Hybrid and Remote. For whichever option you choose, you will also need to provide further details, benefits, pay adjustment, vaccination status etc.

  The Commitments Module showcases five values that you hold dear and gives you room to explain them in more detail and provide links to additional resources. Locations allows you to place your enterprize on one or more locations.

  You can create a Lead Generation Form that has a relevant call to action for visitors to your LinkedIn Page. These currently include Contact Sales, Request free demo, Start free trial and Get Started. You will need to provide a link to your Privacy Policy, a Headline and a 200 character Body Copy description.

You can add up to three Community Hashtags to your LinkedIn Page.

You can also link to Featured LinkedIn Groups (ones that you either Moderate or Participate in and see value in for the Followers of your LinkedIn Page).

You can also choose to have your LinkedIn Page information published in additional languages, which is especially useful if you have a School Page with international students speaking a common language.

- **Send invitations** to Connect with as many current and former employees, stakeholders, VIPs, students and alumni as you can with the goal of securing 60% or more of these people as Followers of your LinkedIn Page. This can be difficult and time consuming for Schools, so I recommend that *from now on*, you invite all students to select your School in the Education section of their LinkedIn Profile before they leave the School with the ultimate goal of securing 80% of students as Alumni. I recommend that this be completed in the second last year of secondary school and as soon as possible or within the first six months of any vocational training, college or university study.

- **Ensure you have at least three LinkedIn Page administrators** this would be the minimum number I would recommend for organizations of more than 10 people to ensure that there is always someone who can update the LinkedIn Page. It is also important to keep a close eye on who has Administrator access and to remove Administrator access when an employee leaves.

8.2 My Employer Tab

The My Employer Tab allows an Administrator to turn on the My Company feature so that employees can connect with colleagues and be informed of the latest company updates. There is a range of information available at https://business.linkedin.com/marketing-solutions/my-company-tab.

As a LinkedIn Page Administrator, you can control what content is visible on the My Employer Tab. Once this is turned on, an Employee can verify their work email address with LinkedIn and access the My Employer Tab when they visit the enterprize's LinkedIn Page.

Likewise, when the employee leaves the enterprize, it would be a good idea in the offboarding process to ask them to remove their work email address from their LinkedIn Profile and put an end date on their employment on their LinkedIn Profile (especially if they are in sales).

If this doesn't happen, or someone else claims to be an employee when they aren't. you can report them to LinkedIn at https://www.linkedin.com/help/linkedin/ask/TS-NFPI.

This is particularly helpful for fake Profiles and impersonators because LinkedIn requires the person to make a counter claim and if that doesn't happen within 14 days, the LinkedIn Page information may be removed from their LinkedIn Profile.

Now is also a good time to go to the Admin Tools Menu and choose the Employee Verification link and add the website name for your LinkedIn Page to the list for the email verification process for Employees. Once added, it cannot be removed but others can be added.

8.3 Content Tab

Here you can find Content Suggestions including Trending Articles, Employee Milestones and Company News.

Trending Articles will provide details of Articles that have been popular over the last 15 days. These may or may not be of interest to your Followers.

Employee Milestones requires your Employees to choose you as their Employer on their LinkedIn Profile and can include details of new hires, anniversaries, or promotions.

Company News will show when your Company is mentioned in the news.

You may also have a 'Recommend to Employees' option that will allow you to recommend content to employees. LinkedIn will find relevant links, photos and videos to recommend to employees. The employees can then share them as original posts on LinkedIn and Twitter.

8.4 Page Statistics, Records And Analytics

If you are in the early stages of developing a LinkedIn Page, I would suggest that you aim for 300 or more Followers and five or more reactions (likes) per Post.

Administrators can invite their LinkedIn Connections to Follow the Page but they can only use 250 credits over a one month time frame. If a person accepts, the credit builds up again.

If you have over 300 Followers, you can choose a Targeted Audience rather than 'Anyone' for your Posts based on Follower profile data including Organization Size, Industry, Jobs Seniority, Geography and Language Preference (without payment). Alternatively, you may like to pay to promote a Post through Campaign Manager https://www.linkedin.com/campaignmanager or Boost your Post (although there is a minimum spend) via the Boost Button on the Post (if it is available for that Post).

If you would like to track your progress over time, these are the Page statistics, records and analytics worth monitoring:

- **Your number of Followers on various dates** to demonstrate how this has improved over time. This is a real time statistic so you will need to keep a manual record of this number, perhaps in your own spreadsheet.

- **The Analytics Tab** will show you how your Page compares to similar enterprizes and location Pages in terms of Followers, New Followers, Posts and Engagement Rates. You can add specific Pages you would like to compare to. You may also like to look at the provided statistics for Visitors, Updates, Followers and Employee Advocacy and ensure that these are continuously increasing.

- **The Activity Tab** provides details on Requests, Comments, Mentions, Posts, Reposts, Reactions and Analytics as well as your Events. As Notifications for your Page do not appear in your personal Notifications Tab, responding to these promptly is important and if you notice a significant drop in engagement, it may be time to increase your Posting schedule and/or adjust your content type and responsiveness to Comments. Personally, I like to host an Event once a month to keep me active on LinkedIn.

- **Review your Competitor Pages** and see what has created engagement or conversions on their LinkedIn Pages. How many Followers do they have and could this be a metric you may like to overtake? It is good to have some big hairy audacious goals.

- **The School Pages Alumni** tab – School Pages allow you to see who has chosen your School, College, Association or University in the Education section of their LinkedIn Profile via the Alumni statistic. This number should be increasing year on year and as mentioned earlier, you should aim to have 80% or more of your current students adding your School to their LinkedIn Profile each year.

8.5 Page Activity

The following is a list of the types of activity you may like to complete that is aligned with your Page.

- **Follow your normal social media strategy or policy guidelines** and make sure your Page activity is similar to your overall social media plans and policies. You may have certain branding or style guidelines, editorial calendars and topics that you need to incorporate when publishing via your Page. Remember to include keywords, hashtags, @mentions, links, pictures, animations, documents, videos, polls, calls to action etc in your updates.

- **Connect with Followers** and reach out to aligned Followers who are not connected to you personally and consider inviting them to Connect to your Personal LinkedIn Profile. If they are already connected to you, now may be a good time to send them a quick personal message with a link to a particular Post that may be of interest. Invite other Administrators to invite selected Connections to Follow the Page as well. Most Administrators will need several reminders to complete this task.

- **Observe Follower behavior** and identify what is happening. Are some of your Followers also Influencers that may like to be personally notified of important updates? Can you reach out to new Followers with a personal welcome message? Can you pass on leads to other areas of the business including recruitment or sales? Can you see who engages with your Posts and reach out to them directly and invite them to Connect to you and Follow the Page?

- **You can respond as a Page** if you are an Administrator of that Page by selecting the Page rather than your Personal Profile from the drop-down box within a Post in the Newsfeed. It is a good idea to respond to all Page mentions with a Comment that is as lengthy and relevant as possible.

- **You can choose to Notify Employees** when a Post has been published (assuming you have Employees and the option is available for that Post) and this can also increase engagement. However, I would recommend that you only do this for important announcements, not every individual Post. If you have more than 300 Followers, you can also send your Post to a Targeted Audience, provided the audience you select using the Language, Job Function, University, Seniority, Region, Location, Company Size and Industry is greater than 300 in total.

- **Videos are highlighted on the menu** when you visit your Page as a User rather than as an Administrator. This gives you an extra incentive to natively upload videos as part of your Page Posts rather than linking to a video hosted on your own website or on YouTube or Vimeo. I have a policy of adding videos to YouTube first (for lifetime value), then editing the subtitles and downloading the .srt captions file so that when I upload the video to LinkedIn, I can also upload the captions so that they appear on the video. Alternatively, use the auto-captions and edit function.

- **Events that are hosted by the Page are listed on the Events tab**. This will show both Upcoming and Past events. People who have registered for those events may also be open to a Connection request and an invitation to Follow the Page or an invitation to a future Event. A quick summary of your events is available via the Events tab on your Page or at https://www.linkedin.com/events.

8.6 Leadership Updates

One of the most challenging aspects of my role as a LinkedIn Specialist working with companies, organizations, schools and universities is convincing the leadership team (including the CEO, Directors, Board Members, Principals and Vice Chancellors) to update their own LinkedIn Profiles.

If you are an Administrator for a Company, Showcase or School Page, you need to ensure that the top end of the enterprize represents the quality of the enterprize as well.

You can lose a lot of credibility if these LinkedIn Profiles are only average in appearance. It is very difficult to convince other employees to update their LinkedIn Profiles if the leadership team have not updated their LinkedIn Profiles. I would also like to encourage you to make sure your own LinkedIn Profile is fully updated too!

Leadership team members can set a good example by including links to the enterprize website in the 'Websites' section and by making sure they Follow the Company LinkedIn Page and are a Member of the relevant LinkedIn Groups (even if they turn off Notifications). They may also be willing to include some additional branding in their LinkedIn Profile Background Banner Image and Media or Links in the Experience section and include selected items in the Featured section.

All of these suggestions can be part of the enterprize Social Media Policy as a list of Recommendations for new employees from day one of their tenure.

8.7 Strategy Reviews

By reviewing your statistics, analytics, notifications, comments and responses, you can update your strategy and tactics for your LinkedIn Page.

Measuring and reporting on these results can drive further development and improvements. Keeping a casual eye on what your competitors and local and international innovators are doing can encourage you to consider what you could incorporate in the future.

I really like capital letter subject headings at the beginning of Posts although this is a personal style technique rather than a requirement because capital letters in online content can be considered as 'shouting.'

Don't forget that LinkedIn is regularly providing new bells and whistles on the platform, so if you schedule time for a review of the LinkedIn Platform every six months. This may also help you find and take advantage of any new Page features.

For example, under the Content tab, you can see Trending Articles, Employee Milestones and Company News and these could be a good source of 'curated' content and save you from having to constantly source good quality and relevant content on your own because the algorithm is doing it for you. However, you would still need to review it before sharing it on your Page.

Remaining current in your selected social media platforms can increase the perception of your enterprize brand. If you are up to date with your digital competency skills, people are more likely to engage with your online content. Please don't be a try hard or a serial pest that uses 'tricks' or 'hacks' to be more visible or sales-focused. These can backfire and have you removed without warning from LinkedIn (another reason to complete regular backups and abide by the LinkedIn User Agreement).

Consistently posting good quality content is much more valuable than posting repetitive sales messages. You may like to include a variety of content that is informative, educational, inspiring, entertaining, engaging and persuading.

Good news items that celebrate achievements of individuals and enterprizes can be well received, provided they are not shared too often and classified as a 'humble brag.' Likewise, being supportive and encouraging of other individuals and enterprizes can be a sign of maturity and authenticity and if it is aligned with your intentions, even better.

Please respond politely to all comments and complaints. If any sensitive content needs to be addressed directly, you can mention publicly that you will contact them directly and privately to discuss the matter further. There is no need to have a public argument, even if you are 'in the right.'

Finally, it is a good idea to encourage employees to be 'advocates' for your enterprize.

When they join your enterprize and are provided with a copy of your Social Media Policy, you can mention that you encourage them to React (Like), Comment and Repost (Share) LinkedIn Page content and provide suggestions on how they can update their LinkedIn Profile and support the enterprize's online activities on various social media platforms.

8.8 Life, Job Advertisements And Business Solutions

A Life tab on the LinkedIn Page can be set up if you apply and pay for a higher level subscription. This is beyond the scope of this book as I am focusing on LinkedIn for you and your career or business rather than LinkedIn for hiring employees or paid solutions.

However, if you would like to publish an individual free or paid Job Advertisement, you can do this at https://www.linkedin.com/my-items/posted-jobs or as a Post in your Newsfeed https://www.linkedin.com/feed (click to start typing a Post and then select 'Share that you're hiring').

Jobs are meant to be 'real jobs' – a paid for your time exchange, not an entrepreneurial opportunity, a commission based role or multi-level marketing scheme. When posting, you must abide by the LinkedIn Jobs Terms and Conditions https://www.linkedin.com/legal/jobs-terms-conditions.

Existing employees, clients, suppliers and stakeholders can be good referrers for people who may like to work at your enterprize. Before you share a job advertisement online, it can be a good idea to share a link to the job with these people first as they may be able to use their LinkedIn network and find someone who may like to apply (either someone they know or someone they search for). It is also nice to give these people the 'first option' and be aware of what is happening in the enterprize before the job advertisement reaches a wider marker.

LinkedIn offers a variety of other paid Business Solutions and access to LinkedIn Partner Products at https://business.linkedin.com, including Sales Navigator. Before considering any of these products, you really need to ensure that everything else in this book has been completed first.

The top brands in the world have more than 60% of their employees on LinkedIn. Imagine how much more effective the paid solutions will be if your employees are supporting your efforts as well.

Also, before you consider using paid LinkedIn Business solutions, please contact a local independent LinkedIn Specialist that genuinely understands your values, purpose, goals and objectives to discuss how you can use the specialist LinkedIn products to achieve results.

Alternatively, ensure that you receive a comprehensive introduction via a LinkedIn salesperson before you purchase any products. It can sometimes be easier to get assistance before you purchase a product rather than after you have purchased a product (and you also want to make sure it will meet your needs effectively before automatically paying for it every month).

If you are no longer using the features, please remember to cancel the subscription because even if you are 'not using it' you cannot claim a refund (in most cases).

8.9 Enterprize Housekeeping Related To LinkedIn

There are plenty of sections to complete and monitor on your Company, Showcase or School Page on LinkedIn. However, you can do a little bit of housekeeping to encourage more people to engage with your LinkedIn Page.

- **Link to LinkedIn on your enterprize website.** I am surprised by how many organizations link to their other social media but not their LinkedIn Page.

- **Add your LinkedIn Profile and/or Page URL link** to your work email signature, business card or your employee profile on the enterprize website etc.

- **Start incorporating your LinkedIn strategy in your everyday work activity** by asking people to Follow the Page, regularly engage with Page content, use your regular hashtags, introduce new staff via Posts, provide Kudos, Endorsements and Recommendations to one another etc.

- **Onboard new Administrators and new employees** – so that they can update their LinkedIn Profile, Follow the LinkedIn Page and engage with the content that is shared.

- **Offboard employees who leave the enterprize** and remind them to update their own LinkedIn Profile with the final month and year of service and remove their Administrator privileges if they are an Administrator. If they have a generic email address attached to their LinkedIn Profile, this will also need to be removed from their LinkedIn Profile i.e. info@companyname.com and you may also want to ask them to remove their work email address from their Profile (especially if they are in sales and going to be selling products for a competitor in the future).

8.10 Employee Engagement And Support

One enterprize client I trained suggested that every employee should cancel their LinkedIn Profile once they joined the business as they should be 100% devoted to his business. I nearly choked on the spot.

Remember, a LinkedIn Profile belongs to the individual person, not their employer and anything an enterprize recommends should be done on a voluntary basis.

There are some employees who do not believe that they should have to do anything to their LinkedIn Profile for the benefit of their employer. I disagree. The success of the enterprize ensures the success of their career and I am more than happy to support an employer who supports me.

Traditional Employee Branding

There are several traditional ways that employees have been supporting their employer in the past:

- Wearing a uniform to work.
- Driving a company vehicle (that may have employer branding on the outside).
- Speaking on behalf of their employer at conferences and events.
- Representing their employer in negotiations, sales and business development meetings.
- Accessing employee benefits, tax discounts, concessions, social club offers etc.

Why wouldn't employees consider supporting their employer online?

If an employer provides clear suggestions, with instructions, on how to support the enterprize via LinkedIn, it is still entirely up to each employee as to whether or not they adopt some or all of the suggestions on their own LinkedIn Profile.

It should not be a condition of employment that a new employee follow the suggestions without question unless it is included in a written employment contract that is accepted in writing before employment commences.

However, I would recommend that every new employee be advised about the Social Media Policy of the enterprize and the compliance requirements before accepting the role and be given a written copy of the Social Media Policy that also explains what they need to do when their employment ends.

Essential Way To Support An Employer On LinkedIn

Most employees, when securing a new role, will update their current role with their new employer on LinkedIn, preferably within one month of starting the position. To be able to do this, the employer must have a LinkedIn Page on LinkedIn and the new employee, when they start typing the name of their new employer in the Company Field when adding the new Experience, will need to select the Company LinkedIn Page from the drop-down box.

Other Ways Employees Can Support An Employer On LinkedIn

There are so many other ways that employees can support an Employer on LinkedIn. These are all optional choices. Some employees may be willing to do more than these suggestions. Enterprize owners should definitely do all of these. These suggestions could come under the banner of 'Employee Advocacy.'

- Use a company branded Background Banner Image behind their LinkedIn Profile Photo (that also looks good on a mobile device when the Profile Photo moves to the center of the screen).

- Provide a brief description of the Company in the Experience Description field (Established in 2001, XYZ organization provides ABC goods and services to DEF customers locally and internationally) and include company keywords in the Job Title and in the Description field.

- Provide a text link to the Company Website URL in the Experience Description field (https://xyzcompany.com) as this appears as a clickable link on an Android mobile device and can by copy/pasted on other devices.

- Provide a video link to a Company Video on YouTube in the Media section for their role or in the Featured section.

- Follow the Company (or School) Page on LinkedIn so that it shows in the Interests section (https://www.linkedin.com/company/XYZCOMPANY).

- Add the Company Website Details into the Contact Details section (https://www.linkedin.com/in/YOURURL/edit/contact-info).

- Add their Company Email Address to their LinkedIn Profile (so they do not accidentally create a duplicate LinkedIn Profile and so that anyone searching for them on LinkedIn via the syncing process will come to their one and only LinkedIn Profile).

- Add the Company Location Address to their Contact Info details.

- Consider incorporating more Company Information in the About section of their LinkedIn Profile.

- Add in any Honors or Awards they have received at the Company in the Honors or Awards section.

- Connect with other Employees at the Company via the People tab.

- Give and receive Recommendations to and from other employees at the Company.

- Give and receive Endorsements to and from other employees at the Company.
- Visit the LinkedIn Page and React (Like), Comment, Repost (Share) or Send Posts from the LinkedIn Page.
- Respond to EDMs (direct emails sent by the Company) requesting you to React (Like), Comment or Repost (Share) an Article or Post prepared by an individual employee of the Company or from the LinkedIn Page.
- Write and distribute an Article that meets the Social Media Policy of the Company that is also search engine optimized and includes links to the Company Website, videos, images, etc. This can be published on either their personal LinkedIn Profile or published via the Company LinkedIn Page if they are an Administrator of the Company LinkedIn Page.
- Encourage other employees to update their LinkedIn Profiles by setting a good example and updating their own LinkedIn Profile.
- Actively engage with appropriate content in the LinkedIn Newsfeed and React (Like), Comment, Repost (Share) or Send items that meet the Company Social Media Policy Guidelines, including @ mentioning and using Company #hashtags where appropriate.
- Editing their Account, Privacy and Communication Settings for maximum effectiveness and efficiency (it could be a good idea to turn off individual email Notifications of various LinkedIn activities).
- Actively researching appropriate information and referrals from the LinkedIn network.

What are the likely benefits of these LinkedIn suggestions?

- The Company website views sourced from LinkedIn may increase.
- The Company brand will be promoted free of charge via employees (sometimes called Employee Marketing or Employee Advocacy).
- When employees update their LinkedIn Profile, they will probably see an increase in LinkedIn Profile views, appearances in LinkedIn Search Results and appearances in online Search Results.
- The Company brand will be more consistent and may attract higher quality talent interested in working for the enterprize.
- Employees will develop pride in their Company association.

- Employees will increase their level of digital competency.
- Statistics for Company Posts, Followers and Engagement will increase.
- Content will have a greater chance of going viral if it receives more Engagement over time.
- If your own digital competency increases, you can teach others.

Now may also be a good time to consider updating the Company Social Media Policy and the LinkedIn instructions for new and existing staff (who may need to complete retrospective updates) and develop procedures for onboarding and offboarding new and exiting employees.

8.11 Company Branding

There is a lot to be said for being on top of the ever-changing LinkedIn Page landscape and really utilizing the options available. As mentioned previously, the best brands in the world have most of their employees represented on LinkedIn. An active Page presence can:

- Showcase innovations and improvements.
- Provide thought leadership from leaders.
- Share news, research findings, employee achievements, career opportunities etc.
- Showcase inspirational actions and results.
- Help manage and respond to a crisis.
- Develop respect and authenticity.

This process requires a firm foundation of quality employee LinkedIn Profiles and a comprehensively completed LinkedIn Page. It develops with quality content that generates engagement, creates new relationships and builds on existing relationships. This ultimately converts into leads, sales and results, whatever a 'sale' or a 'result' looks like for the enterprize.

9. Groups

Groups can be found via the top Work menu or at https://www.linkedin.com/groups. The nature and function of LinkedIn Groups has changed several times since 2003.

In the beginning, without competition from a variety of other social media platforms, or the LinkedIn Newsfeed, well moderated Groups were a fantastic place for like-minded people to come together and share information, ask questions and even vent frustrations and concerns related to the theme of the Group.

Personally, I found the constant Email Notifications too difficult to keep up with, especially as I joined several groups with large numbers of members and with very active participation. Consequently, I turned off the Email Notifications at https://www.linkedin.com/psettings/communications-controls/email.

I did not leave the Groups because I wanted the LinkedIn algorithm to have an idea about the topics I was interested in. The reality is that if I don't actively participate in a Group, I will not gain any tangible value from being in the Group.

A few years ago, LinkedIn appeared to encourage people to spend more time scrolling through the Newsfeed rather than participate in Groups and I can see that their efforts in this area have worked as there has been a significant increase in the overall number of users on LinkedIn and the amount of time a user spends during each LinkedIn session.

As you browse through your own Newsfeed, if you are an active member of a Group (or the Owner or a Manager of a Group), you can consider copying the link to the Post (via the three dots) and post the Link in the Group where you are a Member, Owner or Manager. This can be a good approach for keeping you accountable and active on your own LinkedIn Profile as well as within a Group.

At present, you can manage up to 30 groups at a time and join a maximum of 100 groups. If you exceed the number of groups limit, you'll need to leave one group before you will be able to request to join a new group. You can have up to 20 pending groups and make 20 mentions within one conversation.

A LinkedIn Group can have up to 10 group owners, up to 20 managers and a maximum of two million group members. If you are found cross-posting the same content across multiple groups, it is likely to be identified as spam and will not be posted.

I have seen various individuals and enterprizes start Groups and find it difficult to convince people to join or contribute on a regular basis and some Owners and Managers have had to moderate a lot of sales type posts from people looking to reach a large group of people with one Post.

Some people like to join Groups for research purposes – to find peers in their profession or industry both locally and globally. If the Group Member has authorized it in their Group Settings, you can also message Group Members without being connected to them.

Group Owners and Managers can also Recommend Posts which means that all members can receive a Notification about a Post. This should be reserved for important or particularly valuable Posts. The Recommended Posts are combined in a list underneath the 'Recommended' button at the top of the Groups Newsfeed.

Now could be a good time to review the LinkedIn Professional Community Policies at https://www.linkedin.com/legal/professional-community-policies. It includes a lot of helpful reminders as to what is not appropriate in a LinkedIn Group.

Groups are not a place for self-promotion or for linking to a sales offer. If you do share information in a Group, you can incorporate some reasons as to why it would be helpful for Group Members and include a question to increase engagement.

You can use a variety of Content creation strategies (as outlined in Chapter 11.3) and be supportive of other people's Posts within the Group with Reactions (Likes) and Comments.

If you would like to Repost a Post you see in a Group outside of a Group, you will need to click on the three dots on the top right hand side of the Post, Copy the link to the Post and then paste it into a new Post for your selected Newsfeed (Personal LinkedIn Profile, Company, Showcase or School Page). It may not be visible to someone who is not a Member of the Group.

As a Group Owner or Manager, you can also Invite your Connections to join the Group.

In the interests of keeping the Group vibe consistent, it is a good idea to check the Permissions and ensure that new Posts are approved by an Owner or Manager before publication. You can also decide if you would like the Group to be Open and accessible to everyone on LinkedIn or Closed and Unlisted for a selected group of people.

Posts in Groups can only be viewed by Group Members, so this may help attract some people to Groups rather than the Newsfeed. This makes Groups a good option for Alumni of schools, colleges and universities, provided you can encourage students to join the Group before they leave the educational facility as many will forget to join after they have left, despite repeated invitations. Likewise, if they don't check LinkedIn regularly or they have turned off Notifications, then they probably won't see what has been posted in the Group anyway (but they may find it helpful to see all Group Posts in one location if they do want to check in at a later date and see what has happened over time).

Finally, if you are creating a Group, please include a quality description with 'Group Rules' that make it very clear about the purpose and intent of the Group so you can ensure that the Group experience is positive and rewarding and that the Group Members will engage and gain value from their participation. Ultimately, I believe it is the quality of the Admins and their commitment to the Group that makes a Group worthwhile.

9.1 Group Messaging

An alternative to creating a Group is a Chat Conversation Group that can be created within the Messaging Tab.

You need to be Connected to the person first and then you can add up to 50 Connections to a message. They do not need to be a Connection of other Chat Conversation Group members, just a Connection of yours if you start the Chat Conversation Group. They can also leave the Chat Group if they choose not to be involved.

The Chat Conversation Group can be given a name like 'XYZ Company Sales Team.' Everyone will receive all messages in their LinkedIn messages and they will be grouped under the Chat Conversation Group name (not as individual messages).

This is potentially a more reliable way to keep in contact with a small group of Connections because all messages to the Group will appear in LinkedIn Messages rather than in the LinkedIn Message List. If people check LinkedIn regularly, it means that all messages remain together (unlike an email distribution list). It also means you can scroll back over messages you may have missed due to holidays or other absences.

Anyone in the Chat Conversation Group can remove another member, so if there is an 'Organizer,' it could be a good idea for them to keep an eye on the total number of members in the Chat Conversation Group just in case someone is removed accidentally or on purpose.

These Chat Conversation Groups could be around information updates, specific projects or groups of close teammates, but they do require the Chat Members to be signed in to LinkedIn to see the messages.

Please be aware that in this Chat Conversation Group, every message is sent to every member so if some people are more active than others, it can become very annoying for the quieter members.

I have been a part of two international LinkedIn Specialists Chat Conversation Group for several years and have thoroughly enjoyed keeping up to date with the latest news in relation to LinkedIn from my colleagues around the world. We all share information on a collaborative basis, even though we could be classified as 'competitors' serving similar clients.

This is one of the most enduring aspects of LinkedIn that I really appreciate. Unlike other social media platforms that tend to go through ebbs and flows of popular and unpopular content and activity, the LinkedIn space encourages collaboration, learning and both personal and professional development. Long may it continue.

10. Engaging On LinkedIn

When I first joined LinkedIn, it was very much an online résumé service that allowed you to connect with other individuals from across the world. Back then, we didn't understand the concept of 'individual publishing' that allows our own content to be publicly available without the need to create our own hosted website or online blog.

But things have changed since then – in a big way. LinkedIn is highly optimized for name based search engine queries. Type in almost any name you like into a search engine query and you are more than likely to see a LinkedIn Profile in the first page of online Search Results.

It is also a very powerful publishing platform. I have several LinkedIn Articles that appear at the top of page one of Google Search Results.

10.1 Why Is Engagement Important On LinkedIn?

My second book was all about how to attract the right career or business. I am the sort of person who likes to be clear about what I want and have it come to me rather than try and chase it down. A pull strategy rather than a push strategy. That's not to say I don't go out there and source things that I need or want, but in terms of opportunities, I like to watch my online 'bait' attract the right 'fish.'

When you are an active participant on LinkedIn (I suggest around 20 minutes per week), you are both releasing bait for fish and planting seeds of trust that can grow.

Whether you realize it or not, engaging on LinkedIn can:

- Market you, your enterprize or your cause.
- Develop your brand, reputation or influencer status.
- Inform, educate and entertain readers, viewers or listeners.
- Advocate on behalf of important issues that you engage in.
- Enhance your own learning and content development skills.

Content engagement is a great way to start getting involved, especially if you are a little bit nervous about producing your own content. It will also let other people know that you value their contributions and they will be more likely to be interested in you in the future (which is good for your career or your business).

I encourage you to be mindful and strategic by engaging with the people and Companies that are most aligned with your values, purpose, goals and objectives. If you start liking motivational quotes and bypass all of your profession or industry information, you may miss opportunities.

Curating content is a way to expand your own knowledge base, showcase other people's content and by association, be recognized around the same content themes. If you specialize in a particular niche and share best practice around your topic, you could be very popular indeed.

Creating content may challenge you when you first start, but after some practice, like most things, you will develop and refine your skills and improve. Remember that done is better than perfect (provided you are not irresponsible or plagiarizing without acknowledgment).

Co-Creating content is also an option if you would like extra input from another source. This could be a colleague, a company, a benefactor, a supporter, a collaborator, a client, a stakeholder, a mentor or even an educational institution. Publishing with more than one identity can maximize the use of more than one network in the distribution phase.

Anything that you engage with, curate or create needs to provide other LinkedIn Users with a good experience overall. If you constantly share sales messages, you will quickly notice that they will not generate active engagement and therefore not be seen by many people.

10.2 Engagement Strategies

There are many different ways to engage on LinkedIn.

Did you know that Content within individual LinkedIn Profiles and Articles is indexed and locatable via search engine queries as well?

LinkedIn provides a way to verify your credentials through Skill Endorsements and written Recommendations on your LinkedIn Profile and Kudos Posts in your Newsfeed.

If your Posts and Articles receive a lot of Reactions (Likes), Comments, Reposts and Sends, this is also an indication that you have some online reach.

Your can include audio recordings for your name on your LinkedIn Profile (via the LinkedIn App) and in your Messages.

In the Newsfeed, there are four options to add a Photo, Video, Event or Write an Article. When you click in this box, you will see that there are additional options and you can also add a Document, Share that you're Hiring, Celebrate an Occasion, Find an Expert, Create a poll or Offer your help.

A document could be a PowerPoint Presentation that you have saved as a PDF and then it becomes a carousel of slides). Don't forget that these PDFs can be downloaded by the viewer and seen on a bigger screen. Remember to include a call to action on the last page.

Carousels can also be created via external services like https://canva.com

You can add #hashtags (subject links) and @mentions (alert notifications for individuals or Companies) in your Posts.

You can attend events - check out lots of details at https://www.linkedin.com/events. If you have Creator Mode turned on, you can create your own Events or if you have a LinkedIn Page or you are an Administrator of a LinkedIn Page, you can create Events via the LinkedIn Page.

In various sections of your LinkedIn Profile, you can Upload PDFs, link to Videos or Websites and include detailed Descriptions once the link is accepted.

All of this means that you have a lot of ways to add content and engage on LinkedIn – sometimes too much choice! Consequently there are a lot of people who remain passive observers (lurkers) rather than active participants. Some people have suggested up to 95% of LinkedIn Users do not use LinkedIn effectively.

I am not suggesting that you need to become a regular contributor of new information to be able to use LinkedIn effectively.

The reality is that some of the most productive value comes from supporting others via your Engagement Ratio, determined by how often you engage with other people's content compared to how often you create and share your own content. A suggested good ratio is 12:1. This means that you engage with content 12 times and you share content one time.

I liken this to being one of those encouraging people you may already know that always supports you, no matter what, over many years. Let's call them your Personal Encouragers (PE). They could be a relative, a school friend, a college buddy, a past work colleague or a fellow teammate or hobbyist. They may be older or younger, similar or different. But what sets them apart is that they are willing to encourage you on an ongoing basis. One of my favorite quotes is 'courage beats comfort.' It is much easier to be courageous if you have people in your life who encourage you.

I believe that these PEs are even more important than fans, voters or critics. These PEs are with you during the good times and the bad times. They keep showing up in your life and will turn up if you ask them to and sometimes, even if you don't ask them to. They are willing to tell you how it really is, but their motivation is to support and empower you, not vilify or criticize you.

I attribute most of my success to the love, faith and support of my PEs. Some of these are personal friends and others I call my business friends. If you can't recognize any of these PEs in your life, I encourage you to be a PE and you will quickly realize how wonderful it is to give some personal encouragement to someone on a regular basis. You never know, it could be catching and you may end up with a few PEs of your own!

So how can you provide some encouragement for your nearest and dearest as well as other people in your network on LinkedIn? What can you do that encourages both the LinkedIn algorithm and other people on LinkedIn to help you on your journey?

- Login regularly (once a week is enough) and visit the Newsfeed, Articles, LinkedIn Profiles and Pages according to your values, purpose, goals and objectives.

- Engage with content via Reactions (Likes), Comments, Reposts and Sends.

- Consider connecting with people who engage with Posts that have sparked your interest (I found this very helpful to find and connect with other members of my Professional Associations, in particular, those who engage with the Professional Association Page or Group Posts).

- Endorse people for their Skills.

- Write Recommendations.

- Share a Kudos in the Newsfeed.

- Curate (find) some good quality content already published on LinkedIn, prepare a short summary introduction and share it (with @mentions for the source and #hashtags if appropriate).

- Curate some quality content from another location (with its own link or details) and share it (with @mentions and #hashtag acknowledgments) on LinkedIn.

- Create your own content and Share it in the Newsfeed as a Post (from a LinkedIn Profile or LinkedIn Page).

- Write an Article and Share it in the Newsfeed. You may also like to create an additional Post or message certain people and invite them to engage with it.

- Find people that are aligned with your goals, both locally and internationally, review their LinkedIn Profile and consider inviting them, with or without a personal note, to Connect with you.

I say without a personal note for a Connection Request as some LinkedIn Trainers have found that Connection Invitations without an introduction can perform as well or better than those with a personal introduction! Some people refuse to accept an invitation request without a personal note. I find this to be an unnecessary personal rule.

I REALLY dislike automated or templated Connection requests, particularly if the person has not even looked at my LinkedIn Profile first and asks me something in their Connection request that is clearly stated on my LinkedIn Profile.

Remember that any form of automation is against the LinkedIn User Agreement – and this includes computer generated or human virtual assistant activity generated either locally or internationally.

11. Publishing And Connecting On LinkedIn

There are many different ways to publish content on LinkedIn. We have covered your own LinkedIn Profile and/or Page in great detail. Now we will look at your Posts (in the Newsfeed or Groups), your Articles (via your Profile or Page) and Newsletters.

According to LinkedIn, "Pages that post weekly have five times more followers and grow five times faster than Pages that only post monthly." I have also observed that whilst engagement is vital (listening), you also need to post on a consistent basis (speaking) to maintain your relevance on the LinkedIn platform.

11.1 Content Sharing Ideas

There are many different types of content that you can share, and coming up with ideas can be challenging, especially if you wait until 9:00am every Tuesday and say to yourself 'I need to publish my weekly Post by 10:00am - what will I share?'

Most people find it easier to develop content in blocks, batches or around themes. They may also choose to develop a Content Calendar divided into days, weeks or months with Week 1 have a topic, Week 2 having another topic and so on. With an allocated topic for each week, you can group ideas and themes and produce content much more quickly and reliably.

You need to remember that your content needs to be related to your values, purpose, goals and objectives. If it is to let people know about your expertise, it will mostly be informational, educational and perhaps inspirational.

If you need to achieve specific results, you will need to think about your ideal customers or clients and the various stages they go through - awareness, consideration, decision, retention, advocacy and perhaps even becoming an ambassador.

A lot of people focus their content on awareness and consideration and forget about including a call to action, retaining customers or clients (and maintaining the relationship) or building relationships to the point where you have advocates and ambassadors representing you when they see relevant opportunities.

Here are some content creation ideas that you may find helpful. You may even choose to create your own templates so that you can systemize your content creation and even outsource some of the preparation process (but not the distribution process).

I suggest that you start with a one month and then a three month content calendar and see how it goes before developing a 12 month content calendar. Don't forget to include a variety of formats including images, carousels, documents, polls, audio, video etc.

AIDA – Attention, Interest, Desire, Action (an old sales formula).

How to – top tips, checklists, summary, cheat sheet.

Incentive – free white paper, free class or consultation, product or trial, webinar, infographics, discounts, contests and competitions.

Viral – good quality share, current topic poll, petition, cause for donation, timely viewpoint, humorous (be careful) and informative.

Buzz – news, deadline dates, new releases, exclusives.

Relatable story – that shares a personal experience with some lessons learned or provokes thought and discussion.

Poll – that encourages voting and is quick and easy to engage with.

Open ended question – that prompts the reader to ask themselves the question and respond.

Hypnotic language – that attracts interest. Some words include 'imagine', 'you' and 'because.' These words bypass the conscious mind and create faster engagement. Power words are both persuasive and descriptive and stimulate emotion based on feelings of success, safety, novelty, newness etc.

Recommendations – ongoing, respond ASAP, request.

Awards and Honours – special announcements, significant media (set up Google Alerts so you know when you have been mentioned and can share the media coverage through your networks), acknowledging the generosity or recognition received from others, especially journalists.

Thought Leadership – opinion, research results, survey findings.

Appreciation – acknowledging others in a meaningful, authentic way.

Message sequences – connect with the prospects' pain, need or problem, define the pain even better than they can, discuss what they may have tried and why it hasn't worked, present a solution and explain why it's better, include case studies and testimonials, offer a knockout guarantee, if more than one problem, have a specific message on each, with each message only covering one idea.

Sales message – makes the person look good, saves time, saves money provides value, makes something easier, soft sell, include a question and call to action.

Real time amplification topic – discuss something that is currently 'in the news' provided it has an appropriate analogy and you are not using the issue in a negative way or being insensitive to anyone who may be suffering at the time. Also called 'news jacking.'

Content calendar – align particular topics to different special days or months that you can repeat on a yearly basis, perhaps even creating your own template for your content items. For example, International Volunteer Day or every new calendar year etc.

Curate content – by setting up RSS feeds of top blogs, news agencies, and influencer websites on an RSS reader. This way, you can collect all of your content in one place and select the best to share.

Create content – by using tools like Answer the Public or Google AdWords to explore topics in greater depth. Searching for content on the topic may also give you some good ideas to discuss.

If you are thinking at this point, 'I just want a job,' that is okay. You can focus on developing a good LinkedIn Profile and then connecting with people for the purposes of networking, securing referrals or perhaps even doing voluntary work (my three best tips for getting a job).

However, as soon as a decision-maker digs a little deeper, they will be looking at what sort of content you have shared or what sort of encouragement you have provided or engagement you have completed with other people on LinkedIn. Ultimately, it is not just your LinkedIn Profile information that is used for the recruitment process.

If you are a business owner, you could be thinking that you want to outsource all of this content activity elsewhere as soon as possible! This may or may not work. Ultimately, you are still 'in charge' of the message, and you need to be managing it and making sure that what is published on your behalf is congruent with your values, purpose, goals and objectives, is aligned with your target audience and achieves results!

However, that doesn't mean you have to do everything yourself.

Ways to help you on the content journey include:

- Share a very rough draft of your ideas to a copywriter to build they key thoughts into a longer written piece with relevant citations.

- Provide a detailed briefing to someone else (or a copywriter) to create a draft for your review and editing (remember you know your target audience the best and what they will most want to know).

- Prepare something yourself and then get someone else to review your piece and proof read or modify according to your instructions.

- Develop a template format so that you can rinse and repeat the same style on an ongoing basis (perfect for case studies and speeding up the content creation process).

- Publish your own content but organize someone else to respond to comments and feedback and alert you to any concerns (providing them with a format for each response). This is called community management (but remember, LinkedIn can detect if this is being done from a remote location and may suspend or delete your account).

- Prepare and produce multiple pieces of content and distribute individual segments over time (great for generating traffic back to one or more original pieces).

- Create longer form evergreen content (current today, tomorrow, next week) that you can recycle periodically in long or short form (one piece could be re-used in 10 excerpt-style Posts over several years). You could also diary to review and 'update' once a year.

Please remember that the actual Post area is a maximum of 3,000 characters for a LinkedIn Profile or Page Post. In my view, you need to include something useful within the Post that viewers can enjoy without clicking a link to more information. I often include a shorter summary of what they can find if they do click on a link.

It is also important to think about risk. Personally, I choose not to publish anything that could be perceived as negative, critical or inflammatory. I am solution-focused. You may have other compliance requirements – editorial guidelines, Social Media Policy or industry standards that you need to abide by.

I encourage you to read and understand these principles before choosing to publish any content anywhere. If you need legal advice before publishing, make sure you get it! If in doubt, simply don't publish – just engage, it is still a great way to be noticed.

11.2 Making Posts Go Further

A lot of people love the idea of their Posts going viral. This could be good if everyone who saw the Post did exactly what you wanted them to do (if you are in business) or the right person saw it and contacted you immediately if you wanted work (yeah, right!).

However, that doesn't always happen. Some of the most obscure Posts can go viral and some of the best Posts can disappear from the Newsfeed very quickly and although the algorithm can make a difference, so can a bit of luck.

For example, a key person may engage with the Post and send it viral through their network and this may only happen now and then. Some of my clients ask if I can help them do the same thing twice and I have to admit, I simply can't because it all depends on who sees what and how they respond at each time point.

It can be a blessing if a Post stops going viral because you may have generated so many Comments that if you decide to reply to every Comment, you could be wasting hours of your time and not get any return on your investment and be told off for being non-responsive if you don't reply.

Conversely, if there is something that is very important for you to share, then obviously, the more people who see it in your target audience, the better.

If you plan to use these suggestions with an outright sales message or spammy content (which ruins LinkedIn for everyone), it probably won't work as the LinkedIn algorithm is very good at detecting poor quality content.

Your Post needs to include content that is relevant to viewers of your LinkedIn Newsfeed. Most people can detect a sales message almost instantly and may quickly scroll right past without taking action, even if it grabs their attention at that precise moment, for the right or wrong reason. That is not to suggest you can never sell, you just can't sell all the time.

Also, if you would like to manage your LinkedIn Posts effectively, both your Personal Posts and any Posts you manage on behalf of a LinkedIn Page or Group, you need to keep a list of all of them in your own Content Spreadsheet – Date, Title, Link to Post (from the three dots in the top right hand side of the post), Details and perhaps even an Archive.org/web link to the permanent edition) so that you can quickly access them in the future to either reuse, recycle or perhaps even remove them from LinkedIn if necessary. (See Appendix C)

For example, I worked with a school that posted an old class photo of a group of students and their teacher ahead of the upcoming School Reunion and it turned out that the teacher had been convicted of a criminal offence and was no longer a part of the school. One of the former students saw the Post and immediately contacted the school and asked the school to delete the Post. If the school had easy access to the link for the Post, it would have been an almost instantaneous process.

Alternatively, if the School had been posting and engaging regularly on their School Page, it could have taken quite some time to manually find the Post (content will only appear for a maximum of 12 months so if you don't have the link, it can be impossible to find the Post again unless you get a full data archive which can take a few days). If nothing else, this process of keeping a link to all of your Posts is a risk mitigation strategy. Unfortunately, it will not save you from the person who takes a screen shot of the Post before it is deleted.

Anyway, let's move onto a more positive note. Here are some tips for improving your Posts:

- Start with a catchy reason for reading (topical, timely, terrific) to keep reading – Today, this week, announcing etc. I often include a two to five word topic in capital letters followed by two forward slashes before starting the main content of the Post.

- Provide useful information within the Post (so the reader can gain a benefit without an extra click).

- Include one or more images or a video, or a document (saved as a PDF).

- Make sure your image/s tell a story (preferably your own unique image). If your image can also include a face, text or logo as well, this really helps convey a message visually so even if you don't get a Reaction (Like), Comment, Repost (Share) or Send, you will still secure extra 'dwell time' whilst people hover over the image and read the text. (Make sure you secure the necessary **written** permissions and pay the relevant fees if you are using someone else's image or someone's face, particularly if it is a child's face which would need both caregivers' written permission. Do not use an image you have found on the internet. I absentmindedly did, once, and received a fine from the owner of the image who had found 'their' image by an online reverse image search).

- Alternatively, include a native video (that you upload directly) with a subtitles .srt file (if you upload your video to YouTube first, you can edit your captions and download the .srt file that you can use for your captions). LinkedIn can also provide Auto Captions that you can edit and these captions will be viewable by someone using assistive technology whereas captions burned into the video file may not be able to be read by assistive technology.

- @Mention (also called tagging or pinging) relevant people or Companies in the Post (type @ before their name and choose their name from the drop-down box) so it notifies them and encourages their engagement. For example, if you have won an award, @mention the Award provider, but perhaps also the Sponsor Companies, the announcer, the judges etc. Do not @mention people for potential publicity purposes, especially if they do not have any association with the content, because if they do not engage with the Post, the algorithm will go against you. This is called spam tagging. However, if you do @Mention someone and they Like the Post and make a Comment, it can help you.

- Include a relevant link that adds value to the Post (this is more for the user experience, not for helping the algorithm). Don't try and hide it in the Comments as it is too hard for the viewer to find the link and they will probably move on without clicking it anyway. Don't edit the Post and add it later either. I have heard that you can add a link via the LinkedIn App and you will not be penalized, but I prefer to work from a laptop or desktop device most of the time.

- Include enough white space to make it easy to scan, read or scroll through and understand easily (but do not use broetry - a form of writing that is similar to poetry but extends the length of the Post via very short sentences and paragraphs and feels trite as you read it).

- Include a few appropriate emojis to bring color and life to the Post. This could include colorful ticks or crosses for individual bullet points, graphs, award cups, 100% motifs, symbols etc. Remember that they cannot be understood by assistive technology, so please, don't overdo it!

- Describe what action the viewer could do after reading the Post in the text (politely and respectfully).

- Include three to five hashtags to help LinkedIn add the content to the most relevant hashtag subjects (type # then one word with all characters together. If you use upper and lower case in the #hashtag, text voice readers will pronounce it as individual words e.g.#SueEllson will be read as 'Sue' 'Ellson' instead of 'Sueellson.' I like to include my 'own' hashtag to help aggregate my content via the #SueEllson hashtag).

- Consider including one hashtag that is popular and more likely to generate views of your content (use the search box to see how many followers your hashtag has before you start writing your Post or in a separate tab in your internet browser.

- Secure quality engagement – Reactions (Likes), Comments, Reposts (Shares) and/or Sends from people who are genuinely interested in the content. If posting on behalf of a LinkedIn Page, you may be able to Notify fellow employees of the Post.

- Respond to all Comments as quickly as you can (preferably within 24 hours) and in as much detail as possible too. This helps the algorithm see that the content is valuable as it has generated engagement.

- Provide a thank you Comment or Message to everyone who Reposts or Shares your Post or Article. It takes a bit more effort to see when your content has been shared and you may need to dig to find it.

- Consider messaging some people directly with a Link to your Post (either via LinkedIn or email) and inviting them to contribute in some way (React, Comment, Repost or Send) – you could invite your peers, colleagues, stakeholders etc anyone with a personal interest in the content. This is very helpful to let journalists know that you have shared their story.

- A few days later, revisit the Post and add another Comment to supplement the original Post (another reason to have the Post listed in your Spreadsheet) to help recycle it and maintain its momentum.

- If relevant, a few weeks later, add another Reply or Comment that adds more value and links to content that expands on the original topic and keywords (only for really important Posts). You will have to set yourself a reminder in your calendar or diary to do this.

- Make sure you engage with other people's content as well (not just your own), so that your Engagement Ratio remains at a good level (you Post once, you engage with other people's content 12 times as a rough guide). LinkedIn apparently like it when you Post and then actively engage with the Newsfeed for a period of time straight afterwards.

- Play nice – don't ever be tempted in a moment of aggravation to reply negatively or make anyone else look bad for any reason – firstly, they may unfollow you, secondly, they may always scroll past you in the future (with a negative thought in their mind), thirdly, they may talk badly about you to others and finally, they may Block you. People like it when you are nice to them, not when you are horrible to them! Consider contacting people directly to discuss a matter rather than 'outing' your grievances in public. Doing this by phone or in person is much better than in writing which can be reviewed multiple times and misinterpreted and also used in a court of law.

- Consider the best time to Post for your target audience (local or international) – later in the day may help match another time zones but mixing it up can also catch different people in your network at different times.

- Make an effort to engage with the Content of your biggest supporters and VIPs – take some time out to React, Comment, Repost and Send some of their Content, particularly if it aligns with your target audience. If it doesn't, perhaps pass it on to someone that would benefit from it so you are not always seen as promoting your own Content but you are encouraging people to spend more time on LinkedIn.

- Link to other LinkedIn items in your Post – LinkedIn Profiles, LinkedIn Pages, LinkedIn Articles, Groups etc.

- Consider saving a PowerPoint Presentation as a PDF and adding it as a Document to a Post so that it appears as a slide carousel. You can add a Portrait, Landscape or Square (1080 x 1080 pixels) PDF document of multiple pages and again, a rotating carousel will be available to review the Content on a full screen or to Download directly to a device.

These tips are shared based on my personal experience of using LinkedIn on a very frequent basis since joining LinkedIn on 21 December 2003. I do not have any personal inside knowledge on how the LinkedIn algorithm works. The way it prioritizes content may also change in the future.

At all times, you must consider your values, purpose, goals and objectives, your target audience and your personal or enterprize brand. Remember that consistency is better than perfection, as I have said before. If you can share content once a week for most weeks of the year, you are doing well and will probably be in the top 5% of LinkedIn Users as most people do not share content on a regular basis.

11.3 Video Content

As I have said several times, I have a routine of adding my recorded video to YouTube first, where it can last a lifetime and where I can automatically generate subtitles, edit them and then download the .srt captions file. I then upload the original video and the captions to LinkedIn. YouTube is the second biggest search engine after Google and is owned by Google so it is great for getting extra search engine results. If I am in a rush, I will just link to the YouTube video.

I also believe that video content may be either extremely positive or extremely negative over time. I have seen a female presenter wearing a strapless top on a regular basis with the camera focused directly on her head and shoulders so it actually looks like she is naked in front of the camera. Another male presenter would always stand very assertively in front of the camera and appeared to be shouting. It didn't take long for me to decide to never watch one of his videos again, regardless of the value he shared.

The first three to 10 seconds of your video are critical. If you don't inspire, intrigue or excite people in the beginning, they are likely to stop watching, so I encourage you to put your best content at the beginning!

If the video is going in the Newsfeed, shorter length videos appear to perform much better than long form videos. You may like to experiment with square, portrait and landscape video recording and see which format performs better in terms of reach. I personally prefer landscape as that is how YouTube is mostly viewed although 'Shorts' in YouTube or Reels on Instagram or videos on TikTok need to be filmed in Portrait Mode to provide optimal viewing on a mobile device.

I am a much faster reader than video viewer and as a 'learning junkie,' I can get my 'fix' a lot faster with written or static visual content. However, I also know that other people prefer video that provides moving images and sound. The LinkedIn Algorithm appears to favor different content on different cycles and if a new feature arrives, it seems to have a burst in the beginning.

There is a proverb that says 'familiarity breeds contempt,' so please don't overdo the number of videos you share on LinkedIn because it can potentially be very polarizing and you could end up with a lot more people who either love you or hate you and a lot less in the middle range. Maintaining a video schedule of more than once a month can be personally demanding for some people. That said, I have heard one 'expert' suggest you Post content on social media 7-15 times a day! If I did that, people would hate me!

Ultimately, I recommend including succinct and useful videos as part of a diverse LinkedIn strategy, but not too often as your personal features and style (appearance, voice, language, pronunciation, etc) may distract from your message. Providing a variety of content in different formats is likely to appeal to a wider range of users. Native videos added to a LinkedIn Page are indexed under their own tab on the menu. This can be a great way to showcase your offerings.

If the text you have with the video summarizes the content effectively, it can inspire reluctant video watchers to watch your video, or at least be aware of your main message without skimming past and not playing the video at all.

Personally, I have turned off 'Autoplay Videos' at https://www.linkedin.com/mypreferences/d/settings/autoplay-videos so I need to actually click the play button to watch videos appearing in my Newsfeed so you need to have a good Thumbnail picture as well. The default setting on LinkedIn is to have videos automatically play as you scroll through the Newsfeed.

Some social media platforms allow everyone to produce Live video. At present, this option on LinkedIn requires a third party application integration and most of my clients have chosen to re-purpose video across multiple social media platforms rather than go Live exclusively on LinkedIn.

A service like StreamYard allows you to broadcast on LinkedIn Live, YouTube, Facebook etc simultaneously so if you don't need to 'edit' the content, this may be a good option and can extend the 'life' of your video content beyond a LinkedIn Live viewing on one date and time.

11.4 Search Engine Optimizing Articles

If you are planning to write an Article that can be Search Engine Optimized (SEO) and potentially be found in Search Engine Results, you need to think very carefully about the title of the Article (the most important feature) and create it around something that people will look for in a search query and hopefully doesn't have too much competition already.

It is also important to have relevant sub-headings throughout the Article that are aligned with the main title.

You can start the process by choosing to Write an Article at https://www.linkedin.com/post/new (I realize that this URL says post, but that is just the link!)

To optimize the Article for search:

- Use an amazing title with the most important words at the beginning.
- Use your own image or a royalty free one and add a caption that includes the title of the Article and your name.
- Copy the Title and paste it into the body of the Article, highlight it and change it to Heading 1 font.
- Mention the word 'By' and the name of the Author of the Article and if possible, link to the website or the LinkedIn Profile URL of the Author. I always write and link to 'By Sue Ellson' as this helps Google associate my Author content.
- Prepare some introductory text at the top of the Article (perhaps in italics) to help the reader understand what is coming up (a bit like what you see at the beginning of magazine articles).

- Incorporate sub headings throughout the Article, highlight the text and use Heading 2 font.

- Use various types of markup throughout the Article including quotes, bold, italics, bullet points and numbered points as markup text is prioritized in search results.

- Incorporate links to other content throughout the Article. This can include links to other LinkedIn Articles you have written, other LinkedIn content and external links.

- Include more images and perhaps a video in various locations within the Article to break up the text and provide more visual relief and pause time throughout. Make sure you add Alternative Text for each image (so that people using assistive technology can 'see' the image) and you may also like to overlay an image with a link as well (great if you insert a QR code in your Article).

- Design your own sign off text and links with instructions on what to do next. You may like to type in the Published Date and the Edited Date and encourage readers to Comment or Repost the content by reminding them to do it.

- Copy and save everything you have written on your own device in the unlikely event it is removed from LinkedIn or if you go to Publish the text and it disappears due to a technical fault (this has happened to me several times). Whilst writing your piece, make sure it keeps autosaving as well. Some people prefer to draft their content elsewhere first using more advanced grammar and spell checking services or artificial intelligence tools that can help them prepare a first draft. You do not need to reference an Article as you would an academic piece of writing, but if you are quoting someone, a reference to their name is appropriate.

- From the Publishing Menu you will see a choice called 'Settings.' When you open this, you can add an SEO Title (60 Characters) and SEO Description (160 Characters). Do this before you Publish the Article as you want to avoid making changes immediately after publishing as I have heard this can affect the Article's distribution rate. Complete a final proof read.

- Prepare the introductory text for the Post that accompanies the link to your Article on a separate screen so that when you choose Publish, you can paste in your message (incorporating all of the tips from Section 11.2 about making a Post go further). Select Publish.

- As soon as the Article is published, copy the link to your Article and put it in your Content Spreadsheet with the Date, Title, Link to the Article, Description and Archive.org Link (See Appendix C). You may also like to look at the live Article and make any improvements or adjustments that you didn't see in the creation process. If you can diary for seven days, recording the number of Reactions, Comments and Reposts can also be helpful.

- Copy the link to the Article and paste it into https://archive.org/web and Save the page so that there will be a permanent record of what you have written on the internet in case you lose your digital version. Add this link to your Content Spreadsheet (Appendix C).

- To ensure that the Article gets maximum exposure, create a separate Post that you share from your Personal LinkedIn Profile and/or LinkedIn Page with the introductory text and the link to your Article. Once posted, you can add this Post link to your Content Spreadsheet (Appendix C) as well and track how well it performs.

- Diary to visit the link from your Post and your Article in a week or month and make sure that you have responded to all of the Comments and thanked everyone who has shared your Post or Article.

- Think about your next Article and how you can incorporate any learnings or suggestions for improvement. If you are actively using Articles as part of your LinkedIn Strategy, you could prepare approximately one Article per month. If it is not a key strategy for your needs, you can aim for three Articles per year so that you have some permanent content in this part of your LinkedIn Profile.

For the record, search engines usually only index the first edition of content by date and time of publication as they do not like duplicate content. This means that if you write an Article on LinkedIn under your name, ideally you would not reproduce the content in the exact format on multiple other websites.

However, if it is exclusively your own personal content, you can reproduce it on your own website, which is also wise because if the content is ever removed from LinkedIn or de-indexed from a search engine by LinkedIn, you have your own version accessible online. To be certain that both versions are indexed in search engines, make them at least 30% different. If you add it to your website, copy that link to https://archive.org/web as well.

Be aware that you can publish under your own LinkedIn Profile as well as via a LinkedIn Page.

As you observe the viewing statistics for your Article, be very pleased with your efforts if 10% or more viewers choose to React to your Article because many viewers may read it but not necessarily 'React' to it. For example, 100 Views and 10 Reactions is a good achievement for an Article.

Whilst 'permanent' Articles may not attract as many views as a 'dynamic' Post in the Newsfeed, they are visible indefinitely and can be more effective than your own website for appearing in search engine results, especially if you have a good quality Title and when people visit the Article, they read most of it without going back to search engine results.

Articles that are 'evergreen' in nature (relevant today, tomorrow, next week, etc) can perform very well if you go back to them every so often and update them. You can even re-use the Article link in a new Post at some time in the future.

11.5 Newsletters

Section 7.7.3 goes into detail about how I publish monthly newsletter content on my own website first, then via a LinkedIn Newsletter (in my case via my LinkedIn Profile and my LinkedIn Page) and then I email it to everyone on my email newsletter mailing list. That means I can use the same piece of content four times with just a few formatting updates for each platform.

LinkedIn Newsletters can be search engine optimized in the same way as LinkedIn Articles as they use the same interface. At the top of the screen when you go to Write an Article, you will need to choose whether you wish to publish a Newsletter or an Article.

Ideally, you will be committed to producing a newsletter on a regular basis from either your LinkedIn Profile or your LinkedIn Page.

When LinkedIn Newsletters were first launched, they were promoted widely on LinkedIn, in particular to your Connections and Page Followers.

Once you establish a LinkedIn Newsletter, LinkedIn will invite people who Follow your LinkedIn Profile (or your Page) to Subscribe to the Newsletter and naturally, the more Subscribers or Followers you have, the greater chance you have of people reading each Newsletter you publish.

The priority here is to ensure that your Newsletter content really adds value. There are many different Newsletter styles from the short and sweet narrative to the complex summary of both new and past content.

Making use of markup (Headings, Bold, Italics, Quotes, Lists etc) and including images and videos will ensure that the reader has a more interactive experience and potentially more likely to appear in online search results.

At the bottom of each Newsletter, it will show previous Newsletters you have published, so please make sure that your main Newsletter image at the top of the page is enticing.

For consistency, I have the same Title for each Newsletter 'Sue Ellson Shares Newsletter Edition XXX' or 'Sue Ellson Sharing Newsletter Edition XXX.' However, you can choose to optimize your Newsletter title for online search results. I like having an end of month due date as it keeps me accountable.

Some people have reported that publishing a Newsletter twice a month also works well, but I don't have that much time!

Posts, Articles and Newsletters are used in different ways by LinkedIn, both within LinkedIn and externally in online search results. If you are focused on a career only, you can probably make do with just Posts and Articles. If you are in business, I would definitely recommend Newsletters via your LinkedIn Page and if you are the business as I am, via your LinkedIn Profile as well (but you will need to turn on Creator Mode for your LinkedIn Profile).

You can see (and subscribe to) the Sue Ellson Shares LinkedIn Profile Newsletter at https://www.linkedin.com/newsletters/6869552819440099328/ and the Sue Ellson Sharing LinkedIn Page Newsletter at https://www.linkedin.com/newsletters/7011478630589497344/.

11.6 Connect, Follow and Collaborate

From now on, I encourage you to connect with everyone you meet in person, via email, phone, message etc on LinkedIn. So many people do not actively do this. There are some people you may need to exclude depending on the nature of your work (like patients of medical professionals).

Every time I am contacted by someone new, I see if they are on LinkedIn and I invite them to Connect with me. The only time I do not Connect is if they are not aligned with my values, purpose, goals and objectives or I think they may spam me.

This is an effective strategy for either your career or business. You could include everyone involved in the recruitment process if you are looking for work and everyone who makes an enquiry if you are in business.

This has lead to many future opportunities because my content can appear in their Newsfeed within the first two weeks of connecting and that reminds people of what I do so that if they need me again in the future, they are much more likely to remember me and find me. If they engage with my content in that two week time frame, they may see more of my content on an ongoing basis in the future.

If you Connect with someone at the time of the first interaction, you are likely to be perceived as well-organized. You are 'starting' the relationship immediately rather than following up later when you need something which feels a lot like a sales pitch even if you are only sending a Connection request.

I have also connected with people from the media including journalists, producers and broadcasters as soon as they contact me, publish content or interview me. I imagine that most people contacted by the media do not do this, so this strategy makes me more memorable and gives me a greater chance of being contacted again in the future for more media coverage. I really value being able to educate people through multiple channels.

As I mentioned in Section 2.1, you can use the LinkedIn App Scan Code Feature to do this with anyone you meet in person. This saves carrying a paper business card (although I still have a few of those on hand if I am at a networking event as some people do not have the LinkedIn App on their mobile device).

Other suggestions for people you may like to Connect with or Follow include:

- Fellow Students and Alumni from school or further education.
- Colleagues, co-workers and managers (past and present).
- Funding providers.
- Service providers.
- Friends from any sports, hobbies or interests.
- Family and extended family (very good for early career – includes parents of friends).
- Business friends from your career to industries and professions you have worked in.
- Other members of professional associations where you are a member or would like to be a member in the future.
- High profile people you would like to know now or in the future (not pitch and sell).
- People you have found related to your future goals.
- Individuals that are well known in your profession or industry.
- Local and international people related to the above.

- Companies where you would like to work.
- People you would like to thank or acknowledge, especially if they have shared amazing content.

Connecting to People and Following Pages helps people 'find' you in search results. LinkedIn gives preference in search queries to people you are already connected to (known as First Level Connections) or Pages you Follow. If an in-house recruiter is looking for job candidates, people Following the Company LinkedIn Page are more likely to appear in search results and be favored by the employer as you already have an online connection.

Having a strategy to continually Connect and Follow is essential. You may set some requirements before reaching out. As a general rule, I focus on people based in my country or people in the same industry or profession internationally.

Collaboration can be either informal or formal. You may have some People and Pages that you have clicked the Notification Bell on and you may regularly engage with their content when it appears in your Newsfeed. This is probably the simplest type of collaboration.

The next stage is where you see who has engaged with your content and you consider reaching out directly and inviting them to Connect.

Alternatively, you could see who has looked at your LinkedIn Profile and invite them to Connect (a warm lead). Or look at Second and Third Level Connections who have engaged with your Content.

Completing specific research aligned with your values, purpose, goals and objectives allows you to reach out to very specific People and Pages. You may conduct searches within LinkedIn or externally via a Google Advanced Search as mentioned in Section 2.1.

Whilst I encourage you to find possible collaborators, contacting with them and then pitching to them is not a good idea. Finding someone online is a first step, securing a sale requires several more steps. Alternatively, working jointly with someone requires you to make sure that you are a good fit for one another first.

Sharing information, ideas and values first is essential. Over the years, I have met many other LinkedIn Experts from around the world and as a general rule, we have supported one another's activities. This may not be as common in other industries or professions, particularly when a person or an enterprize perceives you as a competitor.

Personally, I like being connected to possible competitors. In my view, we all service a slightly different target audience with slightly different products and services and I believe that if we all remain agile and relevant, we can all earn a living from the wider marketplace (and I would add, I definitely prefer to work-close-to-home).

We can also cross pollinate and learn from one another with our various initiatives and insights (another reason to Setup, Shine and Surprise).

If you want to reduce the chances of people 'pinching' your Connections, you may like to adjust the Visibility of your Connections (and turn it off) at https://www.linkedin.com/mypreferences/d/settings/connections-visibility. Personally, I like to keep this turned on so that people can verify my authenticity by seeing who else I am connected to and talk to people they may already know to confirm how I work.

Ultimately, you may be able to find collaborators that become advisors, referral sources, strategic partners, joint venture allies or even stakeholders.

Every relationship starts with some form of contact but it is only maintained if you remain accessible. I love the fact that I can meet someone once and be contacted eight years later without paying for any marketing, sales, or advertising during that time (this has actually happened).

I also like being found when I am needed so that I don't have to prospect! I attract (pull) rather than sell (push) to gain opportunities.

12. Jobs And Careers

Research consistently suggests that the best employees are often referred into the enterprize by existing employees – after all, nobody wants to work with someone they don't like! Statistics show that these people are more likely to fit in, understand the workplace culture, be more loyal and stay longer.

However, the world of work is changing. The world of recruitment is also changing. A paper-based résumé sent in a plastic sleeve folder via the snail mail postal system is quite rare nowadays and some employers will exclude applicants who do not have a LinkedIn Profile (which provides a lot more information and due diligence capability than a paper-based résumé).

Many individuals find themselves in situations where their personal context makes it difficult for them to secure full time work or even work that is suitable for their present values, strengths and context. I personally believe that the future will not be job-focused, it will be work-focused based on the skills you offer, although I still live in hope that we can move towards Open Hiring and only require essential skills before giving someone a chance, especially when technology is changing and giving more people access to more options.

Sadly, discrimination still occurs due to age, ability, schooling, gender, sexual preference, ethnic background, local experience level, country of origin, personal beliefs, faith etc.

Securing paid work that matches your values can be difficult if your online story is different to your real world story. If you don't 'tell' your story, how can you 'sell' what you have to offer? If people only read what they see online, is that enough information to make an informed decision about what value you can provide?

The nature of work is also changing, with a huge increase in casual, contract, freelance and gig based work. This can be attributed to many factors such as cost, flexibility, increased use of technology, personal preference and more. Some people do not want to be restricted by a full time job and are choosing to work to live rather than live to work. Regardless of the reasons why work or job seeking is changing, it doesn't stop the need to learn work or job seeking skills.

Remember that most of us have been taught how to do work (or a job), but not how to find work (or a job). Others have been able to secure work or a job, but not necessarily for a reasonable remuneration or commuting distance.

Have you ever considered getting some professional career advice from a Career Specialist? It can save you time and money and ultimately, land you a better opportunity that is more aligned with your values, strengths and context that appropriately acknowledges your worth both now and in the future.

Relying on anecdotes from well-meaning friends and family members can be dangerous. Trying to get free advice from someone with their own agenda may not be helpful either.

Please remember that most recruiters are acting on behalf of the client, not the candidate. Their goal is to place people in roles for a fee and if you do not stay in the position for more than three months, they will need to re-fill the role without an additional fee.

In other words, make sure that if you are developing work or job seeking skills or looking for work related information, you must complete your own due diligence and make sure that the advisor does not have their own agenda.

12.1 Job Seeking Preferences

Before you start searching for work, you can update your Job Seeking Preferences on LinkedIn at https://www.linkedin.com/psettings/#job-seeking-preferences. This includes the Job Application Settings that give you the ability to save or manage any of the résumés you upload to LinkedIn (I still recommend individual Application Documents for each role but I will discuss this in Section 12.4) and the answers to any previously answered LinkedIn job questions.

Sharing your LinkedIn Profile details when you apply for a job is a good idea and you can select 'Yes' at https://www.linkedin.com/psettings/jobs/profile-shared-with-job-poster so that it happens automatically.

You can provide details of your Commuting Preferences at https://www.linkedin.com/jobs/commute-preferences-settings.

You can also 'Signal your interest to recruiters at companies you've created job alerts for' at https://www.linkedin.com/psettings/jobs/job-alerts-shared-with-recruiters and this may be a helpful setting if you don't want to make it obvious you are looking for work to the broader community. It is not entirely private and if your recruiter provides services to your existing employer, you could be 'found out.'

When you apply for some jobs with certain recruiters or enterprizes, you will create an 'account' with LinkedIn. These accounts can be managed at https://www.linkedin.com/psettings/manage-ats-acct.

When you update your LinkedIn Profile with a new role, you can choose whether or not to announce your new role via the notify your Network of Connections selection. This can be automatically set to Yes or No at https://www.linkedin.com/psettings/activity-broadcast.

You may also like to announce your new role via a 'Celebrate an Occasion' Post in the Newsfeed (available after you click in the Newsfeed and then the three dots).

However, it is a good idea if you are updating your LinkedIn Profile in preparation for job seeking, to turn this off in case you accidentally alert people to an update you have completed on your LinkedIn Profile and they inadvertently assume you have changed your job before you have accepted a new position. Once you do have a new position, you may like to turn this setting on and then update your LinkedIn Profile.

On the top of your own LinkedIn Profile, you may have noticed an 'Open to Work' option or a 'Providing Services' option. Open to Work is designed for people looking for jobs or work and Providing Services is obviously designed for people providing services. You can turn on both.

If you are Open to Work you can list five job titles and five locations (perfect for people considering a move to another location in the future). You can also indicate whether or not you are open to Remote Work, Full Time, Contract, Part Time, Internship or Temporary work and make it either visible to everyone or only recruiters. If you make it visible to everyone, you will have a green frame saying 'Open to Work' around your LinkedIn Profile Picture.

If you are Providing Services, you can list up to 10 services and indicate if you are available in one location only or remotely as well and if you would like your Service offerings to be visible to anyone. This setting does not add a frame to your LinkedIn Profile Picture.

More details about Providing Services are at https://www.linkedin.com/services. This could be a fantastic option for people with a side hustle or for people in a career transition phase as well as for people who like doing freelance, contract or gig based work. You can also add some extra details, media files (fantastic for creatives to showcase your work) and request reviews from people you have provided services to.

More information about LinkedIn for Small Business is available at https://business.linkedin.com/grow.

The exciting news is that if you are a Service Provider, people conducting a Search on LinkedIn can select a Service they are looking for in their own Search query. Choose 'All Filters' at https://www.linkedin.com/search/results/people. If you do a Second Level Connection Search, you may be able to find some collaborators or referral sources as well. If you specialize in one area, it is handy to have someone else you can refer to for an overflow of work and vice versa.

12.2 Optimizing Your LinkedIn Profile And Online Presence

If you are looking for a job right now, you need to ensure that you have optimized your LinkedIn Profile for your immediate purpose. I have already explained how to complete your LinkedIn Profile, but there may be some specific areas that need to be addressed immediately.

- **Fully completed** – I shouldn't need to repeat this again, but you really must fill out as many sections as possible, secure Skill endorsements (at least 20 for your top three Skills) and Recommendations (at least six both Given and Received), have an amazing personal Profile Photo and have all of your Contact details accessible so that if someone finds you, they can contact you.

- **Look for career date gaps** – you have various options here. You can leave them unexplained, you can merge roles to cover a longer period or you can provide a description of what happened during the gap in dates

  If there are lengthy gaps and they are unexplained, this could be seen as negative as some people could assume that you were sick, caring for someone, disabled, incarcerated or in some form of legal dispute.

  If you merge roles to cover the to and from dates, you may miss the opportunity to have some big brand name logos on your LinkedIn Profile and the automatic 'connection' with the Company LinkedIn Page Followers and School Alumni that occurs when their logo appears on your LinkedIn Profile. If you want to show continuity, this can be an effective strategy.

  If the gap between roles is longer than three months, you may like to provide an explanation. You don't need to say that you were receiving treatment for a medical illness unless you want to share this information. You can disclose a variety of things you were doing during this time including a work sabbatical, travel, resettlement to a new location, caring for a newborn child (again, not essential), learning new skills, reflecting on your career and next steps, studying, research, writing, job search etc.

  If you had a lot of gaps in employment during the beginning of your career (for example, multiple hospitality roles) and that was more than 10 years ago and the Companies are not listed on LinkedIn, you could definitely merge those dates into one 'Experience' section.

  You may also like to read about the 'Career Break' option in Section 7.9.3 as an alternative way to cover date gaps.

- **Be clear about what you do want** – this may seem obvious, but a lot of people do not describe what they are looking for. Describing your past experience does not explain what you would like to do in the future. Phrases like, 'interested in roles in' or 'open to roles in XYZ industry' or 'looking for an incredible place to work where the team is more important than the individual.' These are all positioning statements that help the reader of your LinkedIn Profile understand where you want to be in the future and what feels like a good fit for you.

- **Make your LinkedIn Profile memorable** – incorporating visual language will help most viewers of your LinkedIn Profile remember some details about you. Describing your values, what is important to you and even your diverse Interests in the About section can make it seem engaging rather than dry and factual. Including a 'Show Reel' video introduction in the Featured section can help people see you on camera. Don't forget the 30 second video you can add via the LinkedIn App behind your LinkedIn Profile Photo.

- **If you have a dark or necessarily secret past** – you can focus on what you learnt or acquired during this time and describe it in keyword focused detail without mentioning names or personal information. You may have completed some personal development or skills-based courses or completed projects that required strong negotiation and teamwork skills. These are all skills that can be transferred into a new job role.

- **If you have been part of a specialist industry for a long time** – for example, a member of the defense force, government, emergency services, etc and are now looking for a civilian role. The goal here is to help viewers understand how you engaged with the rest of business or civilian society and how your skills are relevant for a career outside of that specialist industry. Make sure you explain all acronyms (don't just use initial abbreviations or jargon) and use keywords that are in popular use. Use familiar language at the beginning of each LinkedIn Experience section and use the more complex and industry specific language further down. Explain terminology if needed. When I assisted people in the automotive industry, one person was called a 'Grip Test Engineer.' I had no idea what this meant. When I found out it was a person checking to make sure a new car design would not roll over whilst driving with people of various capabilities, I was very impressed!

- **Update all of your other online content** – this includes all of your other social media, forums and website content. It might be time to untag yourself from certain images that could damage your reputation and remove others that you have posted that do not align with your future direction. Most decision-makers will complete an online search and look at your other social media profiles to see if your LinkedIn story matches your social media story. One person I met had such a wild past in the music industry that she actually changed her name to separate her music lifestyle from her work capability.

- **If you want to change careers** – you need to ensure that your Headline, About and Current Experience sections reflect this new direction. The Current Experience could be temporarily created as a Career Research Role that is in alignment with the change in career you are seeking because the algorithm favors people who have a current position. You can also bring in these future keywords and describe yourself as an 'Aspiring XYZ' or 'Future XYZ' so that you come up in search results for those job titles. You do not have to wait until any additional study or certification process has been completed to help people find you and then read where you are in the process of securing your new role and developing your new skills.

- **Write your content in relevant language/s** – this includes both written language (one LinkedIn Profile in both English and French if you are in France) and the language tone and style for the role or industry with the relevant keywords in the optimum locations.

- **Overcome negative beliefs** – I have met many people who have lost confidence in themselves or their future for a variety of reasons. This can make it extra difficult to decide what to say or not say on LinkedIn. I have seen some LinkedIn Profiles that are nothing more than a rant about injustice. If you are not in a 'good place' right now, it would be very worthwhile to seek some additional support so that you can represent yourself well in the future and either hide or hibernate your LinkedIn Profile now until you are ready to resume the search.

- **Unrealistic expectations** – either too low or too high. Some of my clients and students have had amazing work experience and yet because they have had some time out of the workforce, they tend to sell themselves short and look for very basic part time roles. It worries me. I see this as a waste of their talents when flexible work options are now available. If their expectations are too high, it could be because they have some lofty academic qualifications but not very much on the job experience and they can become disenfranchised very quickly. I encourage people to consider organic growth over time.

Ultimately, the responsibility for sharing your story effectively is up to you, but help is available. I encourage you to make a commitment to your own success.

12.3 Searching For A Job

Once your LinkedIn Profile and online content is optimized, you can begin the job search process.

If you are not currently working, please include an Experience item in your LinkedIn Profile that covers the present date. I believe a lot of recruiters and decision-makers prefer to hire someone who is already working and the search algorithm appears to have a preference for someone who is currently in a role related to their search query. Review Section 7.9 and title your Position as 'Career Research - Keyword, Keyword, Keyword etc' and employer as 'Various'.

LinkedIn provides access to a range of job advertisements via https://www.linkedin.com/jobs. You can Search for jobs, set up Job Alerts so that you can be notified when certain jobs are listed and you can see jobs where you would be a top applicant or that are recommended for you (depending on whether you have a Free or Premium LinkedIn Profile).

When you set up your own Job Alerts, you can also allow LinkedIn to send you Recommendations. If you are currently looking for work, it is a good idea to make use of all of these resources. A majority of job applicants will apply for jobs listed online within the first 24 hours of the publication of the job advertisement as they are already receiving the Job Alerts.

If you have at least 60% of the skills or knowledge to complete a job, it is worth applying for the job, particularly if it is of personal interest to you (either the tasks, the people, the culture or the company).

Likewise, if your bigger goal is to be promoted within a large enterprize, applying for jobs where you have 100% of the skills for a basic job right now is also an option. Once you are working in the organization, you can develop your skills, knowledge and internal networks and apply for a more aligned or senior role when it becomes available.

Applying for jobs advertised on LinkedIn is not the only way to secure work through LinkedIn. On your own LinkedIn Profile, you can mention that you are Open to Work publicly or to recruiters only at https://www.linkedin.com/in/YOURURL/opportunities/job-opportunities/onboarding.

This means that if you have a keyword optimized LinkedIn Profile, recruiters and decision-makers may find you first. If your messaging aligns with their goals, you could be contacted directly and not have to apply for a job at all.

From the Jobs tab, you can also use the Résumé Builder function and complete some Interview Preparation training.

The Résumé Builder uses information from your LinkedIn Profile and it also allows you to edit the content. This could be a great tool for personalizing your Job Applications as each version can be downloaded as a PDF and then uploaded for the specific job you are applying for.

The Interview Preparation tab helps you out with behavioral questions (Tell me about a time when...) that help the decision-maker understand what you have done in the past and decide how that may be relevant for the future. Answering these questions in your head is easy. Asking a friend to sit with you and pose each question and then listen to your answer and provide some constructive feedback can help you practice your possible answers.

If you trust this person, you may like to ask them what they liked and what they would have preferred to hear (not what was wrong). Going through this exercise is a great way to secure some additional feedback. Remember that one person's feedback, particularly if they are close to you, is not the only feedback worth hearing. They may over compensate and either not tell you enough or tell you too much. If you are already feeling a little fragile, let them know that you would like them to focus on the positives rather than the negatives.

Please remember that if they are not an expert in your field or a professional Career Specialist, they may have their own biased opinions based on their own anecdotal experience, so only take what is relevant to your own progress.

Your job search strategy should include **multiple concurrent job search strategies** including:

- Tailor your current Experience role to align with the type of role you are seeking, adding in a 'Career Research' role if need be (not always possible if you are only quietly job seeking).

- Turn on the relevant Open to Work and/or Providing Services choices

- Search for Jobs at https://www.linkedin.com/jobs/search/ and turn on Job Alerts. See your current Job Alerts at https://www.linkedin.com/jobs/jam/.

- Apply for jobs on LinkedIn.

- Connect and engage with people you already know.

- Follow the LinkedIn Page of any companies where you would like to work and look at the Life section on their LinkedIn Page.

- Connect with recruiters that specialize in your industry or profession (and have been in the role for more than three years as they are more likely to have a good network of contacts) and engage with their content.

- Reach out to targeted people for information-finding interviews.

- Ask for referrals from a variety of different people. I have heard of a person getting a job in Australia via a referral from the United Kingdom.

- Review professional association resources and what they recommend for people looking for careers in that field. See if they have a mentoring service and see if you can be matched with a mentor.

- Attend workshops, events, conferences and networking groups (live or online).

- Seek professional advice from a career specialist, coach, adviser, consultant or mentor, etc.

- Complete voluntary work, especially if you do not have any local experience in that location or no experience in that industry or profession.

- Use Google Maps to find local businesses and then Follow them on LinkedIn and Connect with selected staff.

- Be open to short term or temporary options so that you can see what the company is really like before making a longer term commitment.

- Prepare a one page Introductory Letter that summarizes what you can do and provides your LinkedIn URL and contact details, print it out on paper, fold it three times and deliver it to local enterprizes, hopefully close to where you are living to introduce yourself. Repeat the distribution process again two weeks later and then again another two weeks later. People will often keep a sheet of paper but 'lose' a digital message. One person contacted me two years after my first distribution and another person contacted me within 24 hours.

The Introductory Letter is a great way for you to check out an enterprize and for them to check you out on the job without making a permanent commitment.. You may offer to do some temporary, casual or project work or provide a fixed price service. In my case, I was registered as a business and completed the work by invoice at a special rate for the first 50 hours. I quickly realized that it wasn't the best job for me long term, but at least I was paid for the work I completed and we parted as friends. I was called back several years later to provide LinkedIn advice!

If one job search strategy is not working as effectively as you would like, you can try other work seeking skills. Starting one strategy and then waiting for it to work until you start another will waste precious time. Try completing a variety of strategies all at once. In the end, persistence is what counts. Not one strategy over another. Just a consistent commitment to multiple concurrent strategies. You may be surprised to see what happens if you try more than one!

12.4 Applying For Jobs On LinkedIn

In my view, LinkedIn has changed the world of recruitment forever. Since its inception, the number of sales-focused recruiters has significantly decreased, as has the number of online jobs advertisements in newspapers and jobs websites. It is very easy to understand why.

Why would a recruiter or a decision-maker want to write an advertisement, get it approved, place the ad, pay for the ad, receive multiple inappropriate applicants and then have to process them to find a range of average candidates, especially when most of them come from foreign countries and are not suitable for the role?

It is much easier to type in a search query and see if someone with a matching LinkedIn Profile exists and reach out to them directly. Alternatively, finding someone you can ask for a quality referral can save a lot of time and effort. Finding that referral source is a lot easier with a tool like LinkedIn. Even if you don't find an exact match candidate, you can contact someone who may know someone that they can refer to you.

Despite these options, LinkedIn allows enterprizes to advertise jobs and it has the knowledge, based on the content in your LinkedIn Profile, to help you identify jobs that are aligned with your capability and even suggests where you are in the percentile range of applicants for a job (e.g. Top 25% of Applicants).

The 'Easy Apply' option allows you to apply for selected jobs by adding in your résumé as a document or PDF, answering some selected questions, Following the Company LinkedIn Page and pressing apply. Whilst this may make it easy for you to apply, it doesn't help the recruiter or decision-maker understand your suitability unless you personally tailor your résumé to the job description.

As you can only attach one file, I encourage you to edit your résumé so that it is tailored for the role and think of it as an 'Application' Document rather than as a résumé. All of my clients who have followed this Application Document technique have secured an interview. Applicant Tracking Systems (ATS), recruiters and decision-makers appreciate you preparing content that matches their job description. Essentially the first page of the Application Document is a tailored cover letter and the rest is a tailored résumé.

The résumé should list the most relevant skills for the job first. Then for each of your past roles, choose relevant achievements for the role you are applying for and focus on how they can provide immediate value to the employer. I describe this as not being work 'ready,' but being work 'capable.' Most employers expect to see a return on their investment immediately, even if it is not a 100% return on investment on day one of your employment.

It is also important to discuss how you will overcome any differences between your skills and experience and the job description. Using phrases like 'willing to learn more in my own time,' or 'open to peer mentoring' or even 'keen to acquire new skills on the job' can give the decision-maker an understanding of your commitment to providing value as soon as possible. If you say things like 'willing to learn x, y and z' then you will still have those keywords in your Application Document even though you may not have the skills just yet.

Some people get hung up on the length of a résumé and argue about what is too short or too long. In my view, it can be a little longer provided it is 'scan friendly' which basically means, easy to read via a scanning process on either a large screen or a small screen by a person and via an ATS that does it with technology. Multiple keywords in various locations, short bullet points and headings are easier to process than long narratives.

Remember that if you have a very short résumé and you don't include your keywords, you could miss out altogether on having an interview opportunity because you didn't pass the first keyword screening test.

I also recommend that you provide your content in a very simple Word document that includes bold and plain text at 11 point font and avoids italics or underlining (both out of date), columns, tables, text boxes and borders (because the ATS may not be able to read the content within these elements) and keep all of the content consistently formatted (particularly important for past experience) and logical (grouping Professional Skills, Technical Skills, Personal Skills, Industry Experience, International Experience and Interests as suggested for the About section of your LinkedIn Profile).

It should go without saying that the information, particularly the dates on your résumé, need to match the dates on your LinkedIn Profile. Spelling and grammar should be checked both automatically through technology but also by carefully reviewing content before it is sent. Reading it out aloud can help find mistakes that are missed during silent reading.

Some enterprizes link directly to their own enterprize website in the job advertisement and you may need to apply using their own applicant tracking system (not via LinkedIn). This can be time consuming as each applicant system is usually a little different. This is why it is a good idea to have all of your information, certification details, etc, in your LinkedIn Profile so that you can copy/paste any information across. If possible, include the link to your LinkedIn Profile in one of the fields. It is still a good idea to Follow their Company LinkedIn Page even though you will need to do that manually, as they will check you out online and they will be pleased to see that you are already following them. Some enterprizes start the recruitment process by viewing Followers on LinkedIn before anyone else.

12.5 Preparing For Job Interviews

LinkedIn gives you the ability to do some interview preparation at https://www.linkedin.com/interview-prep. You can see sample Questions and Answers and read articles and watch videos on the topic. The 'Succinct, Honest and Engaging' (SHE) method for answering questions is a good tip. You may have previously heard of the Situation, Task, Action, Result (STAR) technique for answering behavioral interview questions (tell me about a time when...).These sorts of activities are great to do with a few trusted friends.

One of the best tips I can share about interviews is to remember that it is not just about them liking you. It is about making sure that you are the right fit for one another. If you are anxious about your personal circumstances, this could come through in your body language and energy levels.

For example, if you are highly stressed or really keen to secure this particular role, you could appear very intense in an interview situation which an interviewer will equate with 'desperate' and you may miss out. Remember that in a negotiation, the person most likely to 'win' is the one who is willing to 'walk away.'

It is easy for me to say just be relaxed and remember that it is their loss if they don't hire you. I am well aware that this is not the reality in every situation.

If you ask the interviewer/s for reasons why you missed out after the interview and reference checking process, they could be true or they could be 'safe' to avoid a law suit. I recommend that you disregard the reason unless there is something there that is truly valuable to you. You need to do whatever it takes to keep applying for work. Having multiple concurrent job search strategies will help you focus on your overall approach rather than what happened in relation to one specific job.

If you develop a negative mindset or beliefs during the looking for work process, this may come across in an interview situation. Unfortunately, it is almost impossible to hide.

You can change the dynamic in an interview situation if you ask questions that make it clear that you want to make sure that the offer is aligned with your values. In one interview, I 'interviewed' the interviewers and believe it or not, they offered me three jobs on the spot!

Asking questions about opportunities for career development, training, progression, mentoring etc can indicate that you are interested in more than the salary or benefits. However, you should still be well versed in how the company operates and all matters relating to the actual position rather than just 'what's in it for me' without completing any research beforehand.

If you know who your interviewers will be, you may like to have a look at their LinkedIn Profiles before the actual interview. You can choose to look at their LinkedIn Profile anonymously if you think it feels a bit creepy. The goal here is to gain insight and understanding into their background so that you can feel more comfortable with the questions and perhaps choose examples that are related to the role you are applying for and also relate to the interviewer's previous work experiences.

If you haven't already, make sure you have reviewed the Company LinkedIn Profile, the items in their Newsfeed and of course their website and other online content via a Google search and other social media. Making it clear that you understand the nature of the company is extremely important in an interview situation, whether it be by automated video, live video or in-person.

Just before the interview starts, please silence your phone and ensure that you will not have any other disruptions if you are being interviewed online (for example, turn of the sound of Notifications you may receive from other Applications).

Near the end of the interview, you could ask if they are open to being connected with you on LinkedIn and then you need to follow up on that. They may be open to connecting immediately if you are meeting in person and you can use the Scan Code feature in the LinkedIn App on your phone, by pressing inside the Search box, then the small icon on the top right hand side of the screen and then use one person's camera and the other person's QR code to connect immediately. If they say no, please respect their choice.

Personally, I like to have a notebook and pen with me during formal meetings as typing on a device can make it appear as if I am completing some other task. If it is an online video, the typing sound can be distracting.

12.6 Accepting A Job

I always recommend that you only say yes to a job offer after you have received a written job offer (email is fine, but not just a phone call). If you are called on the phone and you want to say yes, you can, but you also need to say that you will confirm once you have seen the written offer.

Once that is processed, you can begin to more formally engage with your new employer.

Naturally, you will need to see their Social Media Policy and abide by any of their policies and procedures. They may have guidelines on how to update your LinkedIn Profile, connect with fellow Employees and engage with Company LinkedIn Page updates.

You should not be asked to delete your LinkedIn Profile as this is owned by you, not your employer. If, for security reasons, it needs to be hidden, then you can consider Hibernating your Profile so that you do not lose access to your Connections.

Updating your LinkedIn Profile Experience section should occur as promptly as possible after starting the new job. Some people prefer to wait until they have passed their probationary period. Ultimately, it is up to you.

When you leave a job, your LinkedIn Profile should be updated again, ideally as soon as possible. If you are not moving into another role immediately, you can explain that you are doing Career Research so that the algorithm still believes that you are currently 'working.'

13. Business And Enterprize

Whether you are self-employed or part of a business or enterprize, LinkedIn can help you achieve results.

As I have said earlier, I believe every person can create a LinkedIn Profile and if they are in a business or enterprize, a LinkedIn Page as well.

If you are a solopreneur, in most cases you 'are' the business and although you will be the only 'Employee' listed on your LinkedIn Page, you can still have Followers who are interested in seeing your Posts.

I like having both a Personal LinkedIn Profile (minimum) and a LinkedIn Page. When I post on my own LinkedIn Profile, I also post on my Sue Ellson LinkedIn Page as it keeps a continuous list of what I have published in one place and makes it easier for people to complete their due diligence.

I can also invite my LinkedIn Profile Connections to Follow my LinkedIn Page. When they visit my LinkedIn Page, it is very easy for them to see my free Lead Generation Form and Subscribe to the LinkedIn Page Newsletter.

If you are the owner of a larger business, you can increase your online presence simply by having each employee list their employment details on their LinkedIn Profile. It is important to develop a Social Media Policy for when they start working for you and when they leave. You may like to provide items for their Personal LinkedIn Profile including a suggested Background Image (with the company logo), video links or PDFs to attach as media to their current role and guidelines for the Experience section (including job title, keywords, task lists, company description etc). You may also like to provide instructions on how to connect with fellow employees and explain how you would like them to engage with the LinkedIn Page Posts.

If you are part of a social enterprize, LinkedIn can be a fantastic tool for sharing details of your good works. Just as you would for a business LinkedIn Page, you can ask any employees, volunteers and 'friends' of your enterprize to update their LinkedIn Profiles and engage with your content.

A number of business owners I have met are concerned that completing a LinkedIn Profile will leave staff open to offers from other enterprizes. Yes, this is true. It is also true that this option was around before LinkedIn. Now, we have simply sped up the process. Likewise, it has sped up the process for you to find employees! The best option is to have your employees actively engaged in the enterprize so that they can support your online activities and be as committed to you as you are to them.

13.1 Completing a LinkedIn Page

As mentioned in Section 8, you can set up a new Company or School LinkedIn Page at https://www.linkedin.com/company/setup/new/ and as mentioned earlier, you will need to be listed as a Small Business if you have less than 200 employees and a Medium to Large Business if you have more than 200 employees. If a Company Page has automatically been created by LinkedIn, you can Claim the Page at https://www.linkedin.com/help/LinkedIn/answer/55962/claim-a-LinkedIn-listing-page. It will be a much faster process if you have already added a company email address to your LinkedIn Profile https://www.linkedin.com/psettings/email.

You will be asked to complete the following:

- Company (or Enterprize) name.
- LinkedIn Public URL link you would like – letters and dashes
- Your company Website link (please copy and paste from your internet browser).
- Your Industry.
- Your Company Size.
- Your Company Type (I often recommend 'Privately Held').
- Your Profile Logo (best if 300 x 300 pixels or more).
- Your Tag Line (120 characters).
- Confirm if you are a company representative.
- Supply a LinkedIn cover image (1128 x 191 pixels).

Once your LinkedIn Page loads, you can then add the cover image and complete a 2,000 character Description. Use as many of these characters as possible.

It is very important that this Description looks similar to your website business description and your other social media profiles. It needs to describe what you offer and how you can help your target audience, but also give you room to include as many of your primary keyword as possible.

I encourage you to list most of the information as bullet points as these are more scan friendly (and better suited to reading on a phone). You can also include a Description in other languages which can be very helpful if you have international clients from specific countries that are likely to be reading this information.

You can also include a Phone Number (please write in international format for one click calling) and the Year Founded. Your business can list 20 Specialties and these can again be primary keyword based (again, remember what your ideal clients will be looking for not just what you would like to say).

You can select a Button to put on your LinkedIn Page – either Contact Us, Learn More, Register, Sign Up or Visit Website and again, you can copy the URL Link that you would like viewers to go to.

It is very worthwhile to add a Location to your LinkedIn Page, even if it is only a suburb and nearest city if you work from a home office. Google likes to cross match address information to confirm the accuracy of listings.

You can add three hashtags to your LinkedIn Page. If you have chosen to create a hashtag that identifies your Company Name, then it is a very good idea to Follow it here so you can see if anyone else ends up using it.

You can also Feature Groups on your LinkedIn Page. It would make sense to highlight any that you manage for the business.

If you are creating the Company or School LinkedIn Page for the first time and you work for an enterprize with more than 10 employees, I encourage you to ensure that at least three people can be an Administrator of the page. Once you open the Company LinkedIn Page, the Admin Tools option allows you to add Administrators, provided they are already connected to you. Ideally, you would also ensure that they are Following the Company LinkedIn Page as well.

I hope you enjoyed this more detailed refresher of Section 8! Having a completed LinkedIn Page is always the first step to securing more business and sales from LinkedIn.

If you are more of a solopreneur, don't forget the Providing Services options mentioned in Section 12.1.

13.2 Abiding By The LinkedIn User Agreement - Do Not's

I cannot stress enough the importance of abiding by the LinkedIn User Agreement, especially if you are using LinkedIn for business https://www.linkedin.com/legal/user-agreement. Please read Section 8, the Do's and Don'ts. For now, please re-read the LinkedIn User Agreement and remember:

DO NOT – connect to people and then pitch immediately.

DO NOT – automate (with either tools or people, locally or overseas).

DO NOT – aggravate (keep it professional not personal).

DO NOT – spam (in Connection requests, the Newsfeed through @ mentions, or Messaging).

DO NOT – look for personal social meetings (it is a professional platform, not a dating website).

DO NOT – lie or tell a white lie to achieve a goal (a lie is a lie).

DO NOT – @mention people who are not related to the content in Posts or Images. This is called Spam Tagging because you are usually trying to get more views of your Post. Remember that people who have been @ mentioned can remove the Tag and be very annoyed with you for trying to get free views.

DO NOT – message a group of people you are connected to unless you have permission first (because if one person replies, everyone receives a copy.

DO NOT – humble brag (it is better to include information that is useful for the viewer and/or acknowledges others not just yourself).

DO NOT – discuss politics (it's not the forum).

DO NOT – argue publicly (it's rude).

DO NOT – Post or message people when you are angry or upset. Write down your thoughts and wait until you are relaxed again before you share words that may have unintended consequences (written words can feel harsher than spoken words and can be used as evidence in court).

DO NOT – make vague or bland comments (e.g.'Great post.').

DO NOT – Post frequent sales messages in the Newsfeed (if your content is good enough, people will track you down and ask for the sale).

DO NOT – send sales messages without checking the information on the person's LinkedIn Profile first. Don't ask questions that could have been answered by reading their LinkedIn Profile.

DO NOT – respond negatively to a Post (if you disagree strongly enough and want to say something, discuss it with the person privately first as quite often, abbreviated Post content misses the main point of the message and can be misinterpreted. If it is inappropriate, you can report it to LinkedIn).

DO NOT – get involved in any form of 'Engagement Pod' (where you receive a link and then React, Comment or Repost a Post to create artificial engagement).

DO NOT – pinch someone else's content (plagiarism) and pass it off as your own as it is a breach of copyright. This includes both images and text. Give credit where credit is due.

DO NOT – give your login details to someone else to use (if it is for training support, change it before the session and immediately afterwards).

DO NOT – post boring videos that take more than 10 seconds to get to the point and start adding real value to the viewer.

DO NOT – discuss overly personal information publicly, particularly any information about children or your personal life (there are other social media platforms for personal content).

DO NOT – set unrealistic sales objectives (if you are starting from zero, most social strategies take about six months to start working well on a regular basis. However, once established, they still need to be tweaked over time and offer consistently good quality).

DO NOT – forget about the value of your own up to date and fully completed LinkedIn Profile (and those of your employees) for securing leads, sales and results.

DO NOT – share private information publicly (dates of birth, personal or secure work email addresses unless by consent, phone numbers etc).

DO NOT – cull Connections on a whim. Even if you have changed industries or occupations, people are still people and they know other people and if you are connected to more people, you are more likely to appear in more search results. The only time it may be necessary to cull is if you get close to the maximum number of Connections (30,000). You can have unlimited Followers. If you have a Premium LinkedIn Profile set to 'Open,' so that anyone on LinkedIn can communicate with you via a message for free.

DO NOT – be afraid to purchase a paid LinkedIn Service if you have done all of the 'free suggestions' in this book and you can identify how the paid service can increase sales. Some people try and save the monthly fee but lose thousands of dollars in quality sales. However, you still need to be committed to making use of the paid offerings and cancel the subscription if you are not using it.

DO NOT – explore the paid Sales Navigator or Campaign Manager products without completing adequate training or seeking professional advice. These systems can be optimized, but you will need expert guidance before starting that process.

DO NOT – underestimate the value of hosting regular events for your target audience as the event invitation process ensures that a lot of people see your business and then they get to see you in action and it can be a very high performing pre-sales option if you are in professional services.

DO NOT – assume that LinkedIn is only for white collar professionals working in white collar industries. I have heard stories of a local retailer sharing information about how they operate their business with video insights and customer stories that has created enormous engagement and sales. Likewise, creatives, tradespeople and academics, in my view, are largely under-represented at the moment and they could definitely benefit from a LinkedIn presence.

13.3 Do's On LinkedIn For Business

On the other hand, what you can do is:

DO – invite everyone you meet in person to connect on LinkedIn from now on (unless you don't like them!).

DO – invite everyone you exchange correspondence with to connect from now on (an email exchange can end but a LinkedIn Connection can last).

DO – invite your clients to connect from now on (depending on the nature of your enterprize).

DO – invite selected Connections to Follow your Company LinkedIn Page (with the goal of getting 300 or more Followers but only inviting up to 250 within a month). Constantly aim for an increase in Page Followers.

DO – add a link to your LinkedIn Page on your website and any other social media platforms that give you an opportunity to showcase your other social media e.g. Facebook and YouTube allow you to link to other social media profiles in the online description area.

DO – think about your brand and reputation before you publish anything or send a message. Ask yourself, is this authentically and ethically aligned to my goals and respectful to all users? Unfortunately one negative item can destroy a career or business relationship permanently (if that happens, always be willing to apologize even if the relationship cannot be restored).

DO – personalize any messages you send (you can systemize this process but you must not automate with either technology or people).

DO – engage meaningfully with other people's Posts (make it relevant to the content of the post, including specific words from the original Post and possibly adding helpful commentary or information without stealing the limelight).

DO – recognize and personally thank every fan, supporter, VIP, client, partner, referrer, advocate, ambassador etc whenever you can through @ mentions in acknowledgement or informational Posts, Kudos Posts, Skills endorsements and/or Recommendations or a direct message.

DO – consider group messaging as a 'Conversation' with pre-agreed participants (around information updates, specific projects, close teammates etc).

DO – systemize your processes. If you have a Connection strategy with a follow up Sales strategy, make sure you offer value first before asking for a sale.

DO – triple check any messages you send to people on a repeat basis. I checked one client's prospecting message and had to completely rewrite it. He thanked me later because it achieved a 40% conversion rate.

DO – remember that not everyone logs in to LinkedIn every day, even if you do (some people may not see a 'last minute' offer or invitation until after the deadline has passed). If you are paying for a Campaign, assess how often these people do login and check their Newsfeed or Messages before pressing 'go.'

DO – triple check any Campaigns to ensure that the spelling is correct, the image is aligned and attractive to the target audience and the link is definitely correct and works when clicked (always copy/paste links and check that the link is not to an element of the website page but the entire website page). Click on your ad and double check.

DO – consider hosting Events and adding them as an Event on LinkedIn. They can be in-person or online and you can collect information about the attendees and provide follow up information related to the event. If they agree to further contact (TRUE in the download list of attendees), you can also approach them about your other offerings.

DO – make sure that if people reach out to you that you respond in a timely and respectful manner. Make sure you also diary to follow up.

DO – review your overall strategy but don't rely on just one 'fabulous' result to determine all other marketing efforts. A consistent mix of content types over time is the most reliable approach.

DO – natively upload video with a .SRT captions file, particularly to the LinkedIn Page as these will all aggregate on the Video Tab for the

LinkedIn Page (the video must still be a good, interesting and succinct video).

DO – be authentic and transparent in everything you do and say (if you make a mistake, apologize first, explain second).

DO – help other people save face. If you see someone else has made a 'mistake,' contact them directly, don't shame them publicly.

DO – reach out to people who have looked at your LinkedIn Profile as they are already warm leads (see the last 90 days worth by paying for LinkedIn Premium). You can say thank you for visiting and introduce yourself to Connect and then follow up (but be selective, not everyone will be worth approaching).

DO – invite people who are attending an upcoming event you are hosting to Connect on LinkedIn. You can do this individually with a personalized message or Connection request. Do not overdo this or you will be identified as a spammer by the LinkedIn algorithm.

DO – monitor your Google Analytics and traffic to your website from LinkedIn.

DO – monitor the activity of your competitors and other enterprizes you admire, both locally and internationally.

DO – start with a good personal LinkedIn Profile, then create a manageable weekly schedule (20 minutes) and stick to it. Consistency is better than perfection.

DO – dig deeper if you are in a business development role and look at who is engaging with your content or the content of your competitors. Finding people who might be interested manually can be time consuming. But looking at personally reviewed and selected Second Level Connections of a key center of influence, an individual, other employees, School alumni, or people who engage with a LinkedIn Page Post could help you find aligned people faster.

DO – consider looking for people or organizations that could offer a strategic alliance or a joint venture both in your own country or other countries. These can be far more lucrative than sourcing individual clients from multiple sources.

DO – remove and/or block Connections that cause offence. If their behavior is inappropriate, report it to LinkedIn. If you are concerned for someone's safety, report that too.

DO – ALL of the relevant free options listed in this book before considering purchasing paid services. That includes both LinkedIn

Premium and Sales Navigator. If you want to capitalize on your paid services, the rest of these strategies need to be completed first and you need to be committed to making use of the additional offerings. There is no instant road to success. It is a bit like paying for someone to visit a messy house.

DO – consider adding a LinkedIn Insight Tag to the backend of your website so that you can create more effective paid campaigns with LinkedIn https://www.linkedin.com/campaignmanager (see Account Assets menu).

DO – integrate relevant concepts you have learned from LinkedIn with your other online platforms including your website, social media, online directories, Google Business Account and any other publications related to your career or business.

DO – subscribe to the LinkedIn Marketing Blog at https://business.LinkedIn.com/marketing-solutions/blog to keep up to date with the latest marketing ideas direct from LinkedIn.

13.4 Asking For A Sale

LinkedIn is one of the best forms of social media for Business to Business (B2B) sales and a variety of research studies have said this on a consistent basis over many years.

If we contemplate why, it is easy to understand.

Firstly, people do business with people and LinkedIn gives you direct access to people.

The one marketing technique that has stood the test of time beyond all other methods is word-of-mouth referrals. The LinkedIn Newsfeed reminds you of your Connections, maintains access to your Connections and allows you to find your Connections when you want to either ask them for advice or someone they know for advice.

Ultimately though, to get a sale, a question needs to be both asked and answered. In a negotiation, skilled negotiators aim to convince the purchaser to say 'yes' three times before they ask for a sale.

Now I have tried my best in this book to encourage ethical behavior on LinkedIn and if you are doing any of the wrong things, please, do not ask for a sale.

However, if you are doing all the right things, you will most probably attract sales and all you will need to do is provide the client with the instant ability to purchase your products or services or contact you and then purchase.

In my case, that involves providing links to my website but also having my contact information immediately available. If the future client can do all of their due diligence beforehand, there are no barriers to self-selecting my offering and making a final decision.

If someone has made an enquiry and you have responded, you can (and should) follow up and ask if there is anything else you can assist with or even invite them (and anyone they know) to an upcoming online event that is of interest. Even checking in and providing a helpful Educational Resource will be remembered.

If you identify the person as an ideal client, you can even 'ask for the sale.' Some people manage to do all the hard work and then forget to ask the person if they would like to purchase the product or service.

If you feel slightly uncomfortable asking for a sale, you may find other ways to go ahead. If it is for a service, you could ask, "Would you like me to make an appointment for you this week or next week?" The choice becomes this week or next week rather than yes or no.

If it is for a product, you could do the same thing. "Would you like to purchase it now or place an order for next week?"

If you have these wording options ready (systemized), then you can find a way to overcome any resistance you may have with the selling process.

If you identify them as someone more suitable for another service provider, you can pass them on. This benefits the client, you (avoiding the 'wrong' type of client) and also the other provider who can refer back to you in the future.

In this process, you may find that you give more referrals than you receive. That is okay. It can take time before you know who to pass on work to and when.

Some advisers recommend specializing in a particular niche offering to gain maximum revenue. I am slightly risk averse and prefer to have at least three different channels of income because channels can vary from time to time. When one is up, two can be down, so by having different channels (and a good savings plan), I can ride through quieter times.

It also ensures that I keep learning as there is a tendency, if you do specialize, to become complacent about keeping your skills in different areas up to date. As I also teach, I need to be 'smarter' than the students on a variety of topics and that really keeps me present and engaged in the learning process.

13.5 What Is A Sale?

What defines a 'sale' for you? Is it an exchange of a product or service for payment? Is it the development of an ongoing relationship and multiple sales from multiple sources? Is it the ability to advocate on behalf of a cause? Is it to support the activities of a mission-based enterprize?

One of my students had spent her career in academic research and she left the university and paid AUD$20,000 for a new website to be developed to kick-start her business editing PhD papers.

Why she spent $20,000 on a first edition website I will never know, especially when she did not have a proof of concept or any existing clients. I always recommend an organic 'boot-strap' approach to a new business where as the income grows, so too does the quality of the online presence. I would always explore all of the free options first and build more when my income increased over time.

I encouraged her to find academics on LinkedIn who were 'completing their PhD.' This would have been a very easy keyword search (as many people like to boast that they are completing a PhD) and she could have carefully selected PhD students in disciplines where she has academic editing experience (e.g. science rather than business).

To create a business that would support her monthly expenses, she probably only needed one or two of these PhD students per month. Imagine how much more effective it would have been for her to find these people directly on LinkedIn rather than compete with every other academic editor in a Google Search Engine Result Page?

In her case, she was doubly affected by her location as she was not based in a capital city and would therefore be unlikely to appear in the Google Search Results of most PhD students across the country.

As I see it, she would have been better off starting her business on LinkedIn rather than purchasing a $20,000 website.

14. Review, Revise, Implement

The Surprise Steps include:

1. Review.

2. Revise.

3. Implement new features.

14.1 Review, Revise, Implement For Your Career

If you are focused on using LinkedIn for your career, the review process can involve looking at the career strategies you are using on LinkedIn and assessing whether or not they are working for you.

At a basic level, you will want to be attracting at least 100 views to your LinkedIn Profile per 90 days and at least 50 appearances in Search Results in 7 days.

Hopefully, you will be using multiple concurrent career strategies rather than relying on one strategy before moving on to the next.

These strategies can include:

- Connecting with relevant People.
- Following relevant Pages and reviewing the information there (including the Life section).
- Updating your LinkedIn Profile (Open to Work and/or Providing Services).
- Utilizing the resources in the Jobs section (Job Alerts, Job Ads, Tools etc).
- Applying for Jobs using an 'Application' Document which is a cover letter and résumé in one document.
- Networking and making direct approaches via Research, Groups, Newsfeed etc.

In the revision process, you can assess how these strategies are working for you, reflect on your results, look at what you could improve and remind yourself to follow up with suggested actions listed in this book.

Ideally, you would be keeping yourself up to date with new features available on LinkedIn and exploring these options as well. I regularly share new LinkedIn Features in my LinkedIn Newsletter and on my various social media channels (including YouTube) so please subscribe via the links in the back of this book!

Early adopters often find that if they are using newer features, they will have an advantage over people who are not using newer features. When new features are released on social media platforms, as a general rule, they are given an extra boost of effectiveness to encourage adoption.

However, even a Premium LinkedIn Profile that you pay for will not make up for a badly completed LinkedIn Profile. If your keywords are not there, you will not be found (unless someone personally remembers you and/or refers you).

Many of us enjoy surprises, but we don't want any 'bad surprises' on our LinkedIn Profile. This can include incorrect dates or dates that do not match your résumé, a visible date of birth (part of your identity) or content that reflects badly on you (Posts, Comments, Articles etc). Likewise, if a person cannot reach you easily, you may miss out on being contacted (so don't lock down all of your information and remember to have your email address visible in the first line of the About section).

Surprise can also relate to delight. What can you have on your LinkedIn Profile, in your Featured sections or in the content that you share in Posts and Articles that is insightful, interesting and/or entertaining? Can you present your information in a creative visual way? Remember that most people respond to visual stimuli. Perhaps your introductory video behind your LinkedIn Profile Picture can convey your personality and style? I encourage you to be a courageous character (that is still respectful and ethical).

14.2 Review, Revise, Implement For Your Business

If you are focused on using LinkedIn for your business or enterprize, the review process will require you to look at your statistics and see if they are generating results. You can reflect on:

- Increased LinkedIn Profile Views.
- Increased LinkedIn Page Followers.
- Consistent or increased Engagement with your Posts, Articles and Newsletters including Reactions, Comments and Reposts.
- Consistent or increased Leads - from Lead Generation Tools (from the LinkedIn Page), direct messages and email or phone enquiries.

- Which content performs more effectively (although you will always need a mix of content formats, it is nice to know what is currently trending and use that slightly more often to gain maximum value).
- How are your Employees, Stakeholders, Referral Sources etc engaging with your LinkedIn Posts, Articles, Newsletters, Events, Videos etc and could this be improved?
- Referral traffic to your website from LinkedIn.
- Your consistency - are you engaging with, curating or creating content at least once a week?
- Are you being seduced by the idea of a silver bullet that is perfect in every way? Sadly, it doesn't exist.
- Are you madly implementing every shiny object offering as it appears so that you can appear to be on trend but ultimately skipping the basics and end up confusing your audience?
- Are you tracking your results so that you can see trends but not wasting your time manually collecting statistics that can vary despite similar timing and quality of your content?
- Do you have risk management strategies in place? In particular, your Content Spreadsheet (Appendix C) keeping a record of your Post Links.
- Do you have crisis management strategies prepared?
- Do you have sufficient people involved in the operations and management of your LinkedIn presence? At least three Administrators if you have more than 10 employees.
- Are your brand, marketing, sales, communication and public relations strategies congruent?
- Do the people who manage your social media presence coordinate their efforts with the people managing your website (the only location where you own the content)?
- Are you listening to all stakeholders and adapting your strategies accordingly (not just your target audience)?
- Are you looking to attract a new audience whilst maintaining a relationship with your existing audience and advocates?

In the revision process, you can look at the answers to these questions and any others you may have and where possible, develop some metrics that will allow you to collect qualitative and quantitative information that you can analyze and then select what you will do differently.

You may decide to start with minor testing and tweaks before making larger scale changes. You may also rely on the perspective from several people with different levels of knowledge, skills and experience.

When you make the relevant decisions and select the most important actions for implementation, naturally you will need to follow up again in the future.

It is a very good idea to keep an eye on what your three closest competitors are doing (either locally or internationally). You may be able to complete some basic assessments of their performance and benchmark their results with yours and set some realistic goals you wish to achieve.

I would also suggest that you try and keep on top of the latest LinkedIn strategies for a business or enterprize but also the most current LinkedIn features and benefits.

I regularly share new LinkedIn Features in my LinkedIn Newsletter and on my various social media channels (including YouTube) so please subscribe via the links in the back of this book!

Hopefully your various enterprize strategies will reduce nasty surprises and be responsible for collecting new ideas to surprise and delight. I would definitely encourage a multi-age employee and advisor review as sometimes enterprises can develop a repetitive enterprize voice.

Yes, LinkedIn is a professional network and the content is more business than social and they have excellent monitoring tools to reduce the impact of any bad behavior from spammers, trolls, cybersecurity hackers etc.

There is still room for courageous characters that are respectful and ethical sharing their voice on behalf of an enterprize. Incorporating tools and techniques that were developed or used on other social media platforms may help you stand out and keep your brand identity consistent.

I have seen some enterprizes use LinkedIn for only one purpose, like exclusively hiring new employees and this is a waste. Understanding the value of variou social media is essential and help you meet multiple enterprize objectives and dovetail your LinkedIn activity.

Jumping straight to a 'surprise' option without the review and revision process is dangerous. Enterprizes who make an effort to constantly evolve and grow can achieve the enterprize surprise objective safely.

Incorporating both consistency and variety will keep you both dynamic and interesting.

15. Final Comments

This book has provided you with many options to secure the right career or business, now or in the future. Ideally, it will work best if you know exactly what it is you are trying to achieve first and then work out the best way to do that – whether that is with LinkedIn exclusively or with other online resources.

However, you can definitely start by completing your LinkedIn Profile up to today's date and engaging with the Newsfeed whilst you are clarifying your future direction.

Completing your LinkedIn Profile (and possibly a LinkedIn Company or School Page) can be a good way to reflect on your achievements and skills and help you create your own personalized values-aligned decision-making framework that can be used to choose the best options for you moving forward.

As a gigster using technology to attract aligned gigs, I have become very clear about the work and business I want and the work and business I don't want. This makes it much easier for me to select the best options from the choices I have described in this book.

I am also very aware of the simple lifestyle I would like to live and my personal impact on our precious planet. I feel that my main mission in life is to help people connect and communicate with one another in a meaningful way.

Likewise, I hope this book, 'LinkedIn for me and my career or business' has given you some options for co-creating your own and/or your target audience's future.

I also hope it helps you avoid making any unnecessary mistakes, ending up in LinkedIn jail for inappropriate activity or having your LinkedIn Profile deleted if you have inadvertently breached the LinkedIn User Agreement.

Fortunately, during my association with LinkedIn, I have seen so many wonderful opportunities appear for my clients, students and friends. It has given me the opportunity to help people build their network and secure aligned career and business opportunities.

I am confident that LinkedIn will continue to change and adapt to the changing needs of users and I trust that they will keep a firm hand on the safety and security controls to prevent people from 'killing the goose that lays golden eggs.'

It has been my pleasure and privilege to prepare this content for you and I wish you every success in your future endeavours.

Appendix C in the back of the book provides details of additional resources that may be of interest and Appendix D provides a list of where you can follow LinkedIn on social media and Appendix E provides a list of all of the links that are in the book in the order that they appear.

I have been told that learning with Sue is like trying to have a drink of water from a fire hose. I trust that the value shared in this book exceeds your expectations and that you will recommend it to others and/or write an online review on Goodreads and purchase additional copies at https://120wayspublishing.com.

You may also be interested in reading my first LinkedIn book, '120 Ways To Achieve Your Purpose With LinkedIn.' It provides a range of strategies based on sound principles that you can try.

My other books include '120 Ways To Attract The Right Career Or Business' which is story driven, '120 Ways To Market Your Business Hyper Locally' which is case-study based and 'Gigsters - Any Age or Ability Employees, Experts and Entrepreneurs' which provides a narrative methodology for using technology to attract aligned gigs.

If you have been gifted a copy of this book or borrowed this book from a library, please consider how you can share the benefits and pay it forward to either the author or someone else.

As an author, it is always lovely to receive a thank you message - even better if it includes details of the value of you have received by engaging with the book. You can reach me directly via sueellson@sueellson.com.

Finally, here's to you, LinkedIn and your values, purpose, goals and objectives and ultimately your desired results! I wish you every success using LinkedIn now and in the future!

Appendix A – LinkedIn Profile Information To Collect

Date: ___/___/___

Name: ____________________________________

Speed up the LinkedIn Profile completion phase by collecting your information before filling in your LinkedIn Profile. Happy researching!

Activity 1. Primary Keywords for your Headline and Profile

Words that my target audience will use to search for the value I provide

____

____

Activity 2. Secondary Keywords for your Headline and Profile

Additional words that my target audience will use to find me

____

____

____

____

____

Activity 3: Photo and Background Photo for your Profile

That matches your objective and doesn't distract from your face

____

Activity 4: My Contact Details for your Contact Info

Email addresses present and past, phone number/s, three website links, contact and location details

____

____

____

Activity 5: Main Goal and Summary for your About

Call to action, feature skills or offer, narrative biography

Activity 6: Cool Showcase Items for Featured

Posts, Articles, Links or Media to showcase in Featured

Activity 7: Work Dates, Titles, Organization Names for Experience

Dates, Titles, Company Names, Achievements, Tasks, Descriptions

Activity 8: Training and Education for Education

Course Name, Dates, School, University, Subjects Completed Transcript

____

____

____

Activity 9: Present and past Memberships, License and Certifications

Name, Dates, Item Number, Link

____

____

____

____

____

____

Activity 10: Dates, Titles, Organization Names for Volunteer Experience

Dates, Titles, Company Names, Achievements, Tasks, Descriptions

____

____

____

Activity 11: Top Skills for Skills and Endorsements

General thoughts – still best to choose from available options first 3 – 50

____

____

____

____

Activity 12: People to ask for and give Recommendations

Think strategically and professionally

Activity 13: Membership Details for Organizations

Name, Dates, Item Number, Link

Activity 14: Special Recognition for Honors and Awards

Name, Dates, Details, Link

Activity 15: Items Published for Publications

Can include co-authored items, journals, magazines, books etc

Activity 16: Languages you can use for Languages

And the level of competency

Activity 17: Project Details for Projects

3 projects – Title, Description, Challenges Overcome, Results and Feedback Received, Future Outcomes or Impacts– Professional Focus, Technical Focus, Personal Skills Focus

Activity 18: Courses completed for Courses

Name of course and work experience at the time

Activity 19: Test Scores for Test Score

Details of tests completed and associated scores (if available)

Activity 20: Patent details for Patent

Location and details of patent registration if declaring publicly

Activity 21: Who to Follow for Interests

Influencers, Companies, Groups and Schools to help your Newsfeed

Appendix B - LinkedIn Statistics And Backups To Record

Collect every six months (or monthly if you prefer) - ideally in a spreadsheet with a separate column for each date you collect the numbers. This list shows the link where to find the statistic and the recommended number to aspire to. The seven items marked with an *asterisk are the most important.

Find out when you joined LinkedIn by going to the last page of results at this link https://www.linkedin.com/psettings/data-log

Date joined LinkedIn: ___/___/___

LinkedIn Statistics

1. Number of Connections* (max 30,000)
https://www.linkedin.com/mynetwork
60+ min, 500+ in time

2. Number of Followers* (max unlimited)
https://www.linkedin.com/feed/followers
More than Connections – if significantly more, shows thought leadership and influence

3. Number you are Following (max unlimited)
https://www.linkedin.com/feed/followers
More than Connections – if significantly more, shows where you would like to engage

4. Profile Views last 90 days* (Reverse stalk)
https://www.linkedin.com/me/profile-views
100+ per 90 days

5. Views of your Posts or Articles*
Ideally 1,000+ views per Post
Ideally 100+ views per Article
https://www.linkedin.com/analytics/creator/?resultType=IMPRESSIONS&timeRange=past_7_days
Impressions past 7 Days ______

6. Search Appearances last 7 days*
https://www.linkedin.com/me/search-appearances
50+ per 7 days

7. Number of Featured Skills and Endorsements* (max 50)
https://www.linkedin.com/in/YOURURL
Top 3 20+ votes

Skill 1 Name ______________________________ Votes ___
Skill 2 Name ______________________________ Votes ___
Skill 3 Name ______________________________ Votes ___

8. Number of Recommendations* (Given & Received)
https://www.linkedin.com/in/YOURURL
6+ Received 6+ Given
Received ___
Given ___

9. Number of Reactions (Likes)
https://www.linkedin.com/in/YOURURL/recent-activity
Recommend three or more per week, 10 or more per month and be a strategic 'Personal Encourager'
Reactions ___ last week

10. Number of Comments
https://www.linkedin.com/in/YOURURL/recent-activity
Recommend one or more per week and write as much as possible
Comments __ last week

11. Number of Posts – can be curated, created or co-created
https://www.linkedin.com/in/YOURURL/detail/recent-activity/shares
Recommend one per week or at least, one per month
Posts ___ last month

12. Number of Articles
https://www.linkedin.com/in/YOURURL/detail/recent-activity/posts
Recommend one per month or at least, three per year
Articles ___ last three months

13. Number of Groups you are in
https://www.linkedin.com/groups
Up to you how many but recommend participation in one group per month (or leave)
Group Participation ___ times in the last month

14. Number of Schools or Universities
https://www.linkedin.com/in/YOURURL/edit/education/new
Ensure you have listed all of your education either studying or completed, subjects and relevant keyword topics
Education Providers all listed Yes or No

15. Social Selling Index
https://www.linkedin.com/sales/ssi
Ideally in the top 20% for your Industry and Network
Industry ___%
Network ___%

16. My Network Dashboard
https://www.linkedin.com/mynetwork
Connections ____ (constantly increasing)
Teammates ____ (1 manager, 19 teammates)
Contacts ____ (constantly increasing)
People I Follow ____ (aligned)
Groups ____ (aligned)
Events ____ (aligned)
Pages ____ (aligned)
Newsletters ____ (aligned)
Hashtags ____ (aligned)

17. Hashtags you are Following
https://www.linkedin.com/feed/following/?filterType=channel
Usually recommend less than 20 and adjust according to your values, purpose, goals and objectives
Name of Hashtag ______________________
Name of Hashtag ______________________
Name of Hashtag ______________________
Name of Hashtag ______________________
Name of Hashtag ______________________
Name of Hashtag ______________________
Name of Hashtag ______________________
Name of Hashtag ______________________
Name of Hashtag ______________________
Name of Hashtag ______________________

18. Pages you Follow
https://www.linkedin.com/feed/following/?filterType=company
Follow all of the Companies or Schools where you would like to work or support their activity
Pages ___

19. Influencers, Companies and Hashtags Following
Look for new Influencers, Companies and Hashtags to follow and adjust according to your values, purpose, goals and objectives

All https://www.linkedin.com/feed/following/

Connections https://www.linkedin.com/feed/following/?filterType=connection

Out of Network https://www.linkedin.com/feed/following/?filterType=member

Companies https://www.linkedin.com/feed/following/?filterType=company

Hashtags https://www.linkedin.com/feed/following/?filterType=channel

20. Newsletter Subscriptions
https://www.linkedin.com/mynetwork/network-manager/newsletters
Review your list and see if you want to remain on the mailing list (suggest top 50)
Name of Newsletter ______________________________
Name of Newsletter ______________________________
Name of Newsletter ______________________________
Name of Newsletter ______________________________
Name of Newsletter ______________________________
Name of Newsletter ______________________________
Name of Newsletter ______________________________
Name of Newsletter ______________________________
Name of Newsletter ______________________________
Name of Newsletter ______________________________

Feel free to add in any other statistics - like how many newsletters you have published or LinkedIn Lives you have run etc.

LinkedIn Backup

Adjust your Internet Browser to 'Ask where to save downloads' first!
Collect every six months or more often if you are very active on LinkedIn.

1. Backup your Profile by Saving to PDF
https://www.linkedin.com/in/YOURURL

Visit your Profile and click on the 'More' Button and choose 'Save to PDF' (from More Options below Headline)

Save file with the format

YYYYMMDD-Your-Name-LinkedIn-Profile.pdf

Once downloaded, copy and save any other details that do not appear in the PDF document.

You can also save the LinkedIn Profile of other people on LinkedIn by completing the same steps.

2. Getting a copy of your Data (the works)
https://www.linkedin.com/psettings/member-data

6 monthly minimum – when you receive the email from LinkedIn, click on the link and save the Zip file immediately. You can open the CSV file in LinkedIn with all of your Connections – First Name, Last Name, Current Job Title, Current Company, Date Connected. Inferences file is also very interesting.

Appendix C - Content Spreadsheet Columns

Keeping a record of the date, topic, link and archive link of all of the Posts you have added to the Newsfeed in a Content Spreadsheet can be helpful for many reasons.

It can be a risk management, crisis management and marketing review tool. It allows you to calculate your consistency rate, your performance rate and you can have information on standby to re-use at a later date.

You can set the date and frequency of when you follow up and decide if you will collect the total number of views, reactions, comments and reposts. It is up to you!

On my website at https://sueellson.com/latest-offer, I provide free access to a range of files that are ready to use for keeping social media records and statistics.

The LinkedIn Content Spreadsheet Columns for either your LinkedIn Profile and/or LinkedIn Page can include the following across the top of each of your columns.

Date

Post Topic (Brief Description)

Post Text Content (if you want to keep a record) *Optional

Post Link (URL)

Posted By (name of person if not you)

Notify Employees (yes or no) *Optional for LinkedIn Page

Content Format (image, document, video, poll etc) *Optional

Archive.org/web link (URL)

Special Notes

You would then repeat the following four columns as often as needed - I would probably diary for one week after Posting and one month after Posting.

Date	Impressions	Reactions	Comments	Reposts
Date	Impressions	Reactions	Comments	Reposts
Date	Impressions	Reactions	Comments	Reposts

Appendix C – Content Spreadsheet Columns

Appendix D - LinkedIn Resources

- **About LinkedIn** – latest statistics and information on LinkedIn https://about.linkedin.com
- **LinkedIn News Pressroom** – includes resources for journalists and details of special journalists program https://news.linkedin.com and https://news.linkedin.com/media-resources/linkedin-for-journalists
- **LinkedIn Safety Center** – includes various information and suggestions for staying safe online https://safety.linkedin.com
- **LinkedIn Mobile App** – where you can download it for either your Apple or Android device from the App Store or Google Play https://mobile.linkedin.com
- **Blog** – the official LinkedIn Blog https://blog.linkedin.com
- **Talent Blog** – is another LinkedIn Blog that specialises on topics related to talent, careers, recruitment etc https://www.linkedin.com/business/talent/blog/topics
- **LinkedIn Premium (for individuals)** – where you can learn more and gain access for one month for free (remember to cancel at the end of the month if you don't want to keep paying) https://premium.linkedin.com
- **LinkedIn for Small Business** – information, free and paid services for small business https://business.linkedin.com/grow
- **LinkedIn Business Solutions Site Map** – provides a list of products, solutions and resources offered by LinkedIn https://business.linkedin.com/sitemap
- **LinkedIn Talent Solutions** – information, free and paid services for attracting and recruiting the right talent. Encourage you to receive as much training as possible from LinkedIn Sales Staff before purchase https://business.linkedin.com/talent-solutions
- **LinkedIn Talent Training** – for people considering using LinkedIn Talent Solutions https://training.talent.linkedin.com
- **LinkedIn Marketing Solutions** – business to business marketing offerings including access to LinkedIn Ads. Encourage you to

set up with an expert https://business.linkedin.com/marketing-solutions

- **LinkedIn Marketing Training** – suitable for people considering advertising on LinkedIn https://training.marketing.linkedin.com

- **LinkedIn Sales Solutions** – find out what paid services you can access including Sales Navigator (for business) https://business.linkedin.com/sales-solutions-b

- **LinkedIn Sales Training** – suitable for people considering LinkedIn Sales Solutions and definitely encourage you to receive as much training as possible from LinkedIn Sales Staff before purchasing their solutions https://training.sales.linkedin.com

- **LinkedIn Learning** – access a range of short courses that can be added to your LinkedIn Profile (free with a LinkedIn Premium Subscription) https://learning.linkedin.com

- **LinkedIn Brand** – where you can download the LinkedIn logo and read the brand guidelines https://brand.linkedin.com

- **LinkedIn Careers** – information on how to work for LinkedIn https://careers.linkedin.com

- **LinkedIn for Higher Education Professionals** – for students, alumni, careers and marketing https://university.linkedin.com

- **LinkedIn Talent Training** – suitable for people considering using LinkedIn Talent Solutions - definitely encourage you to receive as much training as possible from LinkedIn Sales Staff before purchasing https://training.talent.linkedin.com

- **LinkedIn Opportunity** – skills, jobs and interview information and resources https://opportunity.linkedin.com

- **LinkedIn Recruiter** – information, free and paid services for hiring people https://business.linkedin.com/talent-solutions

- **LinkedIn Sales Navigator** – information and paid services for lead generation https://business.linkedin.com/sales-solutions/sales-navigator

- **Certified Marketing Partners** – if you need extra help with the LinkedIn products and services, LinkedIn can direct you to relevant partners https://business.linkedin.com/marketing-solutions/certified-marketing-partners

- **My Company Page Experience** – provides employee experience strategies https://business.linkedin.com/marketing-solutions/my-company-tab

- **Developers** – where you can integrate LinkedIn features with your other online initiatives – probably most useful for the people helping you with your website and data integrations or if you would like to create an App that utilizes LinkedIn https://developer.linkedin.com

- **API Terms of use** – information on how the LinkedIn API key can be used https://legal.linkedin.com/api-terms-of-use

- **Engineering** – provides details of how LinkedIn engineers work and what they are working on https://engineering.linkedin.com

- **LinkedIn Directories** – these can be viewed without being logged in to LinkedIn and the lists are for People, Companies, Schools, Jobs, Learning, Services, Posts, Articles, Newsletters, Products and Salaries sorted in alphabetical order
  https://www.linkedin.com/directory/people
  https://www.linkedin.com/directory/companies
  https://www.linkedin.com/directory/schools
  https://www.linkedin.com/directory/jobs
  https://www.linkedin.com/directory/learning
  https://www.linkedin.com/directory/services
  https://www.linkedin.com/directory/posts
  https://www.linkedin.com/directory/articles
  https://www.linkedin.com/directory/newsletters
  https://www.linkedin.com/directory/products
  https://www.linkedin.com/directory/salaries

- **LinkedIn Accessibility** – information on how LinkedIn is made accessible https://www.linkedin.com/accessibility

- **LinkedIn Help** – comprehensive help library https://www.linkedin.com/help/linkedin where you can also access Live Chat

- **Contact LinkedIn** – https://www.linkedin.com/help/linkedin

- **Help Ticket** – for you to lodge a ticket directly with LinkedIn https://www.linkedin.com/help/linkedin/solve/contact

- **One Click Personal Profile Follow Link Format URL** – for you to replace sueellson with your own personalized URL https://www.linkedin.com/mynetwork/discovery-see-all/?usecase=PEOPLE_FOLLOWS&followMember=sueellson

Appendix E - LinkedIn Online

I encourage you to Follow LinkedIn on your favorite social media channels.

LinkedIn https://www.linkedin.com/company/linkedin

Facebook https://www.facebook.com/LinkedIn

Instagram https://www.instagram.com/linkedin

TikTok https://www.tiktok.com/@linkedin

Twitter https://twitter.com/linkedin

YouTube https://www.youtube.com/user/LinkedIn

or https://www.youtube.com/@linkedin

You may also like to read some of the back story on **Wikipedia**

https://en.wikipedia.org/wiki/LinkedIn

Appendix F - List Of Links In This Book

Please replace the text YOURURL with your own LinkedIn URL that you would have edited from firstname-lastname-lettersandnumbers to your unique URL at https://www.linkedin.com/public-profile/settings.

The links are listed in the order that they appear in the book.

https://120wayspublishing.com/books/book-reviews-of-LinkedIn-for-me-and-my-career-or-business

https://www.goodreads.com/sueellson

https://g.page/sue-ellson-author/review

https://sueellson.com/reviews

https://sueellson.com/courses

https://sueellson.com

https://www.linkedin.com/mypreferences/d/two-factor-authentication

https://www.google.com.au/advanced_search

https://www.linkedin.com/legal/user-agreement

https://www.linkedin.com/psettings

https://www.linkedin.com/psettings/communications-controls

https://www.linkedin.com/psettings/email

https://www.linkedin.com/psettings/phone

https://www.linkedin.com/mynetwork/settings/manage-syncing

https://www.linkedin.com/psettings/account-preferences

https://www.linkedin.com/psettings/member-data

https://www.linkedin.com/mynetwork

https://www.linkedin.com/feed/followers

https://www.linkedin.com/me/profile-views

https://www.linkedin.com/analytics/creator/?resultType=IMPRESSIONS&timeRange=past_7_days

https://www.linkedin.com/me/search-appearances

https://www.linkedin.com/in/YOURURL

https://www.linkedin.com/in/YOURURL/recent-activity

https://www.linkedin.com/in/YOURURL/detail/recent-activity/shares

https://www.linkedin.com/in/YOURURL/detail/recent-activity/posts

https://www.linkedin.com/groups

https://www.linkedin.com/in/YOURURL/edit/education/new

https://www.linkedin.com/sales/ssi

https://www.linkedin.com/mynetwork

https://www.linkedin.com/post/new

https://www.linkedin.com/feed/following/?filterType=company

https://www.linkedin.com/feed/follow

https://www.linkedin.com/feed/following

https://www.linkedin.com/feed/following/?filterType=connection

https://www.linkedin.com/feed/following/?filterType=member

https://www.linkedin.com/feed/following/?filterType=company

https://www.linkedin.com/feed/following/?filterType=channel

https://www.linkedin.com/mynetwork/network-manager/newsletters/

https://www.linkedin.com/psettings

https://www.linkedin.com/in/sueellson

https://www.linkedin.com/public-profile/settings

https://www.linkedin.com/public-profile

https://www.linkedin.com/psettings/account-preferences

https://www.linkedin.com/public-profile

https://www.linkedin.com/psettings/account-preferences

https://www.linkedin.com/psettings

https://www.linkedin.com/psettings/browse-map

https://www.linkedin.com/psettings/email

https://www.linkedin.com/psettings/phone

https://www.linkedin.com/psettings/two-step-verification

https://www.linkedin.com/psettings/profile-visibility

https://www.linkedin.com/psettings/privacy/email

https://www.linkedin.com/psettings/connections-visibility

https://www.linkedin.com/psettings/presence

https://www.linkedin.com/psettings/activity-broadcast

https://www.linkedin.com/psettings/communications

https://www.linkedin.com/psettings/message-preferences

https://www.linkedin.com/psettings/data-privacy

https://www.linkedin.com/psettings/advertising-data

https://sueellson.com

https://NewcomersNetwork.com

https://CamberwellNetwork.com

https://www.google.com.au/advanced_search

https://www.linkedin.com/public-profile/settings

https://www.linkedin.com/in/YOURURL/opportunities/job-opportunities/onboarding

https://photofeeler.com

https://www.linkedin.com/in/YOURURL/detail/contact-info

https://business.google.com

https://www.linkedin.com/in/YOURURL/opportunities/job-opportunities/onboarding

https://www.linkedin.com/psettings/twitter-accounts

https://www.linkedin.com/mynetwork/network-manager/newsletters

https://www.linkedin.com/company/setup/new

https://www.linkedin.com/search/results/groups

https://www.linkedin.com/in/YOURURL/edit/secondary-language

https://www.linkedin.com/psettings/select-language-for-translation

https://www.linkedin.com/company/setup/new

https://www.linkedin.com/help/linkedin/ask/TS-NFPI

https://www.linkedin.com/campaignmanager

https://www.linkedin.com/events

https://www.linkedin.com/my-items/posted-jobs

https://www.linkedin.com/feed

https://www.linkedin.com/legal/jobs-terms-conditions

https://business.linkedin.com

https://www.linkedin.com/company/XYZCOMPANY

https://www.linkedin.com/in/YOURURL/edit/contact-info

https://www.linkedin.com/groups

https://www.linkedin.com/psettings/communications-controls/email

https://www.linkedin.com/legal/professional-community-policies

https://canva.com

https://www.linkedin.com/events

https://www.linkedin.com/mypreferences/d/settings/autoplay-videos

https://www.linkedin.com/post/new

https://archive.org/web

https://www.linkedin.com/newsletters/6869552819440099328

https://www.linkedin.com/newsletters/7011478630589497344

https://www.linkedin.com/mypreferences/d/settings/connections-visibility

https://www.linkedin.com/psettings/#job-seeking-preferences

https://www.linkedin.com/psettings/jobs/profile-shared-with-job-poster

https://www.linkedin.com/jobs/commute-preferences-settings

https://www.linkedin.com/psettings/jobs/job-alerts-shared-with-recruiters

https://www.linkedin.com/psettings/manage-ats-acct

https://www.linkedin.com/psettings/activity-broadcast

https://www.linkedin.com/services

https://www.linkedin.com/search/results/people

https://www.linkedin.com/in/YOURURL/opportunities/job-opportunities/onboarding

https://www.linkedin.com/jobs/search

https://www.linkedin.com/jobs/jam

https://www.linkedin.com/interview-prep

https://www.linkedin.com/company/setup/new

https://www.linkedin.com/help/LinkedIn/answer/55962/claim-a-LinkedIn-listing-page

https://www.linkedin.com/psettings/email

https://www.linkedin.com/legal/user-agreement

https://www.linkedin.com/mynetwork/import-contacts

https://www.linkedin.com/campaignmanager

https://business.LinkedIn.com/marketing-solutions/blog

https://120wayspublishing.com

https://about.linkedin.com

https://news.linkedin.com/media-resources/linkedin-for-journalists

https://safety.linkedin.com

https://mobile.linkedin.com

https://blog.linkedin.com

https://www.linkedin.com/business/talent/blog/topics

https://premium.linkedin.com

https://business.linkedin.com/grow

https://business.linkedin.com/sitemap

https://business.linkedin.com/talent-solutions

https://training.talent.linkedin.com

https://business.linkedin.com/marketing-solutions

https://training.marketing.linkedin.com

https://business.linkedin.com/sales-solutions-b

https://training.sales.linkedin.com

https://learning.linkedin.com

https://brand.linkedin.com

https://careers.linkedin.com

https://university.linkedin.com

https://training.talent.linkedin.com

https://opportunity.linkedin.com

https://business.linkedin.com/talent-solutions

https://business.linkedin.com/sales-solutions/sales-navigator

https://business.linkedin.com/marketing-solutions/certified-marketing-partners

https://business.linkedin.com/marketing-solutions/my-company-tab

https://developer.linkedin.com

https://legal.linkedin.com/api-terms-of-use

https://engineering.linkedin.com

https://www.linkedin.com/directory/people

https://www.linkedin.com/directory/companies

https://www.linkedin.com/directory/schools

https://www.linkedin.com/directory/jobs

https://www.linkedin.com/directory/learning

https://www.linkedin.com/directory/services

https://www.linkedin.com/directory/posts

https://www.linkedin.com/directory/articles

https://www.linkedin.com/directory/newsletters

https://www.linkedin.com/directory/products

https://www.linkedin.com/directory/salaries

https://www.linkedin.com/accessibility

https://www.linkedin.com/help/linkedin

https://www.linkedin.com/help/linkedin/solve/contact

https://www.linkedin.com/mynetwork/discovery-see-all/?usecase=PEOPLE_FOLLOWS&followMember=sueellson

https://www.linkedin.com/company/linkedin

https://www.facebook.com/LinkedIn

https://www.instagram.com/linkedin

https://www.tiktok.com/@linkedin

https://twitter.com/linkedin

https://www.youtube.com/user/LinkedIn

https://www.youtube.com/@linkedin

https://en.wikipedia.org/wiki/LinkedIn

https://www.linkedin.com/psettings/data-log

https://120wayspublishing.com/contact

https://www.linkedin.com/newsletters/6869552819440099328

https://www.linkedin.com/newsletters/7011478630589497344

https://sueellson.com/contact

https://sueellson.com/latest-offer

https://120wayspublishing.com/books/book-reviews-of-linkedIn-for-me-and-my-career-or-business

Index

This index was manually created to give you direct access to many important topics in this book. If you have a digital version of this book, you can search for topics by keyword.

The index quotes Section Numbers rather than Page Numbers.

Author

Sue Ellson BBus MPC CDAA ASA WV SPN

Sue Ellson is an Independent LinkedIn Specialist, Author, Educator, Career Development Practitioner, Consultant, Founder, Gigster, Trainer, and Poet who likes walking and dancing.

Sue was born in Adelaide, South Australia. Sue moved to Melbourne in Victoria, Australia in 1994. She has two adult children. Sue enjoys the simple pleasures of life, especially breathing fresh air.

Sue has completed a Bachelor of Business in Administrative Management from the University of South Australia (2000) unisa.edu.au, is a Member of the Melbourne Press Club MPC (since 2008) melbournepressclub.com, is a Career Development Practitioner and a Member of the Career Development Association of Australia CDAA (since 2015) cdaa.org.au, a Member of the Australian Society of Authors ASA (since 2015) asauthors.org, a Member of Writers Victoria WV (since 2018) writersvictoria.org.au and the Small Press Network SPN (since 2019).

Sue has a varied range of professional experience in banking, training, recruitment, career development, human resources, marketing, networking, online publishing, social media and business.

Sue's first enterprize, Newcomers Network was started in 1999 and her first website newcomersnetwork.com went live in 2001. Newcomers Network and Sue's close circle of local and international friends have helped her understand the needs of people from many different cultures and countries.

Sue joined LinkedIn on 21 December 2003 and she has been consulting, training, speaking, writing and advising on the topic of LinkedIn since 2008. In 2012, she created Camberwell Network which she hosted until 2022 and in 2015, she created 120 Ways Publishing 120wayspublishing.com. Sue has been attending many online and in-person educational events every week since 2000 to keep herself up to date. In 2016, Sue wrote and published three books:

'120 Ways To Achieve Your Purpose With LinkedIn'
'120 Ways To Attract The Right Career Or Business'
'120 Ways To Market Your Business Hyper Locally'

In 2019, she published 'Gigsters - Any Age or Ability, Employees, Experts and Entrepreneurs' which was a finalist in the Australian Career Book Award. In 2023, she published 'LinkedIn for me and my career or business.'

More information about Sue is online at sueellson.com
LinkedIn connections welcome at LinkedIn.com/in/sueellson
Reviews welcome at sueellson.com/reviews

Sue Ellson - Topics

Sue is most passionate about:
> helping people live a values-driven meaningful life (career or business)
> utilizing LinkedIn and technology to achieve a purpose
> the successful settlement of newcomers, expatriates and repatriates
> the value of local communities and becoming more connected

Sue Ellson - Speaking and Training

Sue welcomes opportunities to be a keynote speaker, presenter or trainer at conferences, seminars and professional development events in Australia and overseas. Her previous presentations are listed at sueellson.com/presentations

Sue Ellson - Consulting

Sue provides personally tailored individual and group consulting services online and in Melbourne, or with sufficient notice, in person elsewhere depending on availability. Her current services and pricing are listed at sueellson.com/services-and-pricing

Sue Ellson - Publications

Sue has written a variety of articles for many different publications and welcomes selected opportunities to provide exclusive written content. Her previous publications are listed at sueellson.com/publications, poems at sueellson.com/poems, videos at sueellson.com/videos and audio at sueellson.com/podcasts-audio-and-radio-programs.

Sue Ellson - Media Requests

Sue has provided a range of content to newspapers, magazines and online publications and has been a guest on radio programs, podcasts and television both in Australia and overseas. More information at sueellson.com/about.

Contact Sue Ellson

sueellson@sueellson.com
info@120wayspublishing.com
LinkedIn.com/in/sueellson

Subscribe

Sue Ellson Shares LinkedIn Profile Newsletter at
https://www.linkedin.com/newsletters/6869552819440099328

Sue Ellson Sharing LinkedIn Page Newsletter at
https://www.linkedin.com/newsletters/7011478630589497344

Copyright

Photocopying and reproducing in print or digital format

If recommending the content in this book to friends, family, clients or colleagues, please keep in mind that the original rights belong exclusively to the author, Sue Ellson. The content has been generously provided and it is only fair that the reward be returned to the author to recover the cost of research, writing, production, distribution and future editions.

If you wish to reproduce, store or transmit any part of this book, please email the publisher info@120wayspublishing.com for written permission rights. All quotations need to be referenced to Sue Ellson

---

Follow The Publisher
https://120wayspublishing.com/contact
LinkedIn, Facebook, Twitter, Instagram, YouTube

Follow The Author
https://sueellson.com/contact
LinkedIn, Facebook, Twitter, Instagram, YouTube, TikTok

Latest Offer and Free Downloads
https://sueellson.com/latest-offer

Reviews Welcome
https://120wayspublishing.com/books/book-reviews-of-linkedIn-for-me-and-my-career-or-business

Made in the USA
Monee, IL
05 November 2026

67815668R00134